The

Metal Craftsman's Handbook

An Illustrated Dictionary of Metalworking

Developed by the . . .

**AMERICAN ASSOCIATION
FOR VOCATIONAL
INSTRUCTIONAL MATERIALS**

Engineering Center
Athens, Georgia 30602

The American Association for Vocational Instructional Materials (AAVIM) is a nonprofit nationwide organization supported by universities, colleges and divisions of vocational education in all the 50 states and several provinces in Canada. Each state/province has a vested interest in the organization such that the work actually becomes a part of its own efforts.

AUTHOR and ILLUSTRATOR

William T. Squires, Assistant Professor, Visual Arts Department, University of Georgia

GRAPHIC DESIGN

George W. Smith Jr., Art Director, AAVIM

EDITOR

J. Howard Turner, Editor, AAVIM

1980

ISBN 0-89606-050-0

Printed in the United States of America

Contents

Preface

This handbook is designed to supplement the metals area of instruction. It will provide a ready reference for teachers, students and other individuals who are working with metals.

The author, AAVIM staff, and specialists who contribute to the production quality of this work are to be congratulated.

AAVIM is proud to add this excellent aid to instruction to its list of offerings.

W. Harold Parady
Executive Director, AAVIM

Introduction

The quality and beauty of the craftsman's work is always a reflection of his knowledge, skill and sensitivity. The precise form his ideas take may be strictly utilitarian or purely aesthetic, but the quality and uniqueness of his work is always built upon a basic knowledge of his craft. This handbook furthers knowledge of metalworking through explanation and definition of terms. It is designed to promote craftsmanship founded upon a basis of accurate and unambiguous information.

Verbal definition of metalworking tools and terms may be accurate, however they are often difficult to visualize. For this reason, vision and understanding are aided by the use of illustrations. Pen line drawings were chosen for their summary expressive qualities. The drawings are simple, direct and free from extraneous detail. Their purpose is to clarify the text.

This is a general reference work for artisans, sculptors, hobbyists, teachers and students of metalworking. It will meet specific informational needs of the beginners as well as the experienced craftsman. Fundamental metalworking terms, tools and materials are identified and explained. For anyone new to metalworking, tool use and identification is a problem. This work will familiarize the novice with tools and their characteristic uses. For the professional, much of the terminology encountered in metalworking literature is defined.

In an age which publishes and purchases handbooks and dictionaries by the pound, this small volume should provide the user a welcome relief. Its condensed size should make it a handy studio and shop reference. Like all lexicons, this work lists items in alphabetical order. When several fall under a single generic name they are so listed. Cross references are included under the specific name: PEWTER (See: BRITANNIA). The illustrations are placed immediately after, or within, the pertinent entry.

William T. Squires

5

Acknowledgments

The assistance of several individuals was noteworthy during the preparation of this work. Sheila S. Squires offered valuable help with technical research and organization. Dr. Victor Nix very generously placed his personal library at the author's disposal. Ms. Bonnie Boothe worked untiringly on preparation of the original typescript. Mr. Frank Ruzicka and the Department of Art of the University of Georgia provided the author time and encouragement for this project. The editorial staff of the American Association for Vocational Instructional Materials made every effort to satisfy the author's desire for a quality presentation of his work.

ABRASIVES:

Sharp crystalline particles formed of various natural or synthetic materials which are marketed in the form of grinding wheels, discs, surfaced paper or cloth and powders (i.e. emery or pumice) whose main purpose is to wear away metal surfaces, edges, etc.

ABRASIVE BLASTING:

A wet or dry metal cleaning or finishing process. During this process an abrasive powder is blown against the metal by compressing air through a nozzle. This method both chemically and mechanically cleans metal.

ABRASIVE CUT-OFF SAW:

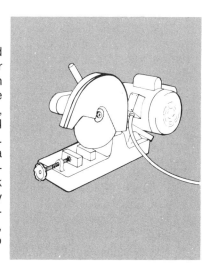

This is a bench-mounted manually operated power cutting machine which uses an aluminum oxide abrasive wheel for rapid, rough cutting of metal pipe, tubing and bar stock. The saw operator, using a hand lever, lowers the cutting blade onto the stock which is to be cut. By exerting an even, downward pressure on the lever, the operator is able to make his cut.

ABRASIVE PAPER:

A durable paper or cloth to which particles of emery, flint, garnet, carborundum or similar materials have been adhesively bonded. Used for finishing and polishing.

A. C.: (See: ALTERNATING CURRENT)

ACETYLENE:

A highly volatile hydrocarbon gas ($HC=CH$) used as a fuel for soldering, welding and for cutting metals. It is colorless, and possesses a characteristically unpleasant odor.

ACETYLENE PRESSURE-ADJUSTING SCREW:

A thumbscrew having a large round or flat-sided head. It is used to regulate gas pressure for welding. Clockwise turning increases gas pressure which should never exceed fifteen pounds per square inch.

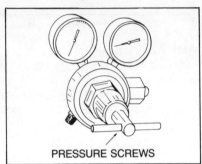

PRESSURE SCREWS

ACID-CORE SOLDER:

Acid-core solder is a soft hollow core wire solder which is manufactured on spools. It varies from other wire solders in that it has a liquid flux-filled center. As the solder is melted and deposited, the flux removes any oxide film coating the metal and thereby promotes bonding of solder with metal.

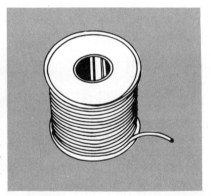

ACME THREAD:

The sides of the Acme thread have a twenty-nine degree included angle, while the top and bottom of the thread is flat and very similar in form to the square thread. Acme thread screws are used for feed and adjustment purposes on machine tools.

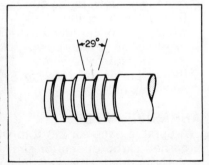

8

ADHESION BONDING:

A chemical fastening of metals using either thermoplastic, thermosetting or elastomeric adhesives. These chemical adhesives bond metal parts by diffusing into the surface where molecules of the adhesive material produce an attraction between the metal and the joint. A strong joint is formed when a catalyst is applied or added and the adhesive material solidifies.

AIR-ACETYLENE WELDING:

A process wherein fusion is achieved by heating surfaces to be joined with a torch which combines acetylene under pressure and air. The air-acetylene flame is typically used for hard soldering and brazing of light metals. Filler rod metal may or may not be used.

AISI:

This is a designation which stands for the American Iron and Steel Institute, which uses code numbers that indicate the composition of a very complete listing of steel alloys. AISI numbers also cover a wide range of stainless steel.

ALLEN SCREW:

A cap or setscrew having a hexagonal socket in the head. These screws are used extensively in machine shops and on office machinery.

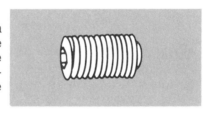

ALLEN WRENCH:

A hexagonal, L-shaped key used for tightening cap or setscrews which have recessed heads.

ALLOY:

Iron is a base or "pure" metal. An alloy is "impure" in the sense that it is a composite metallic substance made up of a base metal and at least one other metal or non-metal. For instance, brass is an alloy of copper and zinc, while steel is an alloy of iron and carbon.

ALMANDITE:

A deep red variety of garnet used for abrasive coatings on paper and cloth. It lacks the toughness of silicon-carbide or aluminum oxide and is most often used for wood finishing.

ALNICO:
This is an alloy of cobalt, nickel and aluminum from which small permanent magnets are made.

ALTERNATING CURRENT (A.C.):
An electric current that reverses direction at regular intervals. Abbreviation — A.C.

ALUMINUM:
A lightweight metal and the earth's most plentiful, it comprises eight percent of the earth's crust. It is mined in the form of bauxite ore which consists of aluminum oxide, water, sand and oxides of iron and titanium. Friedrich Wohler discovered aluminum in 1827, but only since World War II has aluminum become a widely used construction material. Aluminum is difficult to weld, and most aluminum welding is done by the Tungsten Inert Gas (TIG) process. Aluminum has advantages over carbon steel in that it weighs only 25 percent as much and is more resistant to corrosion.

ALUMINUM BRONZE:
Copper alloys which contain between 4 percent and 10 per cent of aluminum; in addition, they sometimes include small percentages of iron, nickel, tin, or manganese.

ALUMINUM JOINT PREPARATION:
Preparation of aluminum joints for welding is approximately the same as for steel. Plate heavier than one-quarter inch should be beveled. An added precaution against weld cracks in aluminum is the addition of notches along the edges of both square and vee joints.

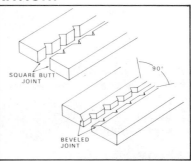

SQUARE BUTT JOINT

BEVELED JOINT

90°

AMALGAM:
The name given to any alloy of mercury with another metal.

AMERICAN SCREW GAGE:
A standard of measurement against which machine screw diameters may be checked.

AMERICAN STANDARD WIRE GAGE (AWG):

A numbering system which is used to give specific information about wire sizes. The exact gage of bare, solid wire may be determined by inserting it into different slots until it "fits." Gage numbers are printed next to each slot.

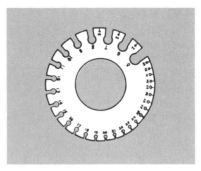

AMERICAN WELDING SOCIETY (AWS):

Organized in 1919, under the leadership of its first president, Dr. Comfort A. Adams, the AWS successfully set uniform standards for welding performance. The AWS has continued its efforts at standardization of electrode and filler metal rod specifications and welding procedure.

ANGLE:

A common structural steel shape having two legs of equal or unequal length which intersect at 90 degrees.

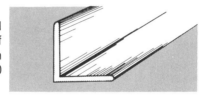

ANGLE RAISING:

One of several metal raising techniques, this procedure involves holding a disk of sheet metal at an angle against a T-stake as it is hammered and turned.

ANNEALING:

The heating and slow cooling of metal in order to make it less brittle. Process varies according to whether metal is ferrous or nonferrous.

ANODE:

The positive pole of an electrolytic cell, usually the supply source of the metal being deposited during the plating process.

ANODIZING:

The coating of aluminum with a protective film by the use of an electrolytic oxidation process.

ANTI-FRICTION METAL: (See: BABBIT)

ANTIMONY:

A hard, silver-white metallic element having a crystalline structure. It is most frequently used in alloys of tin and lead to provide hardness.

ANVIL:

A steel-faced iron block upon which metal parts are shaped, formed, bent, fractured, and joined by hammering and heating.

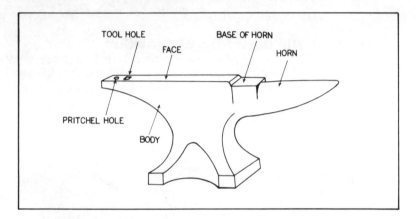

ANVIL VICE:

A vise whose stationary jaw is shaped like an anvil and may be used like an anvil for light metal forming. (See: VISE, MACHINIST'S)

API:

Steel specifications relating to pipe and sponsored by the American Petroleum Institute.

ARBOR:

A revolving shaft, axle or spindle which holds such rotating tools as milling cutters.

ARC:

(In Electric Welding):

A visible flash of electricity which spans the gap separating the work lead (electrode) and the work (ground).

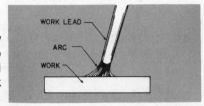

ARC BLOW:
Deviation of an electric arc from its normal path caused by magnetic forces in the weld metal.

ARC CUTTING:
Arc welding processes may be adapted for cutting metal. The voltage regulator on an arc welding machine is turned up well above the proper setting for welding and the intense heat of the arc is used to melt away areas of metal. Arc cutting has the disadvantage of being rough; it lacks the smoothness of flame cutting.

ARC GOUGING:
Use of the arc to cut a beveled edge.

ARC VOLTAGE:
Voltage which spans the welding arc.

ARC WELDING:
A group of metal joining processes during which fusion is accomplished by heating with an electrical arc. Both alternating current (A.C.) and direct current (D.C.) are used. Pressure may be applied; filler metal may or may not be used.

ARGON:
Gas used as a shielding atmosphere during fusion welding. The addition of oxygen to argon during welding results in improved weld penetration and a reduction of spatter.

ARKANSAS OILSTONE:
A light colored, natural stone quarried in the Ozark Mountains which gives a fine edge to steel cutting tools.

ASME:
The American Society of Mechanical Engineers specifies steel, but in most instances their numbers are the same as ASTM specifications.

ASTM:
The American Society for Testing Materials is an organization which sets specifications including a number of different types of steels. Their specification is always prefixed by ASTM.

AVIATION SNIPS:

These snips utilize compound leverage at a 12 to 1 power ratio for cutting light gage sheet metal with much less effort than conventionally designed snips. The blades are constructed of heat treated and hardened steel with serrated edges or teeth. These snips are designed for making straight cuts. Two other designs are available for making right or left curving cuts. Aviation snips cut most types of metals and cut thicknesses of metal up to 20 gage.

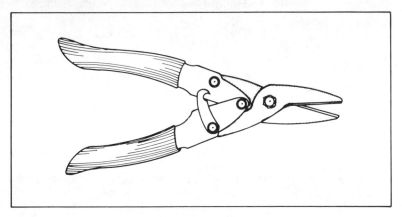

AWL: (See: SCRATCH AWL)

AWS: (See: AMERICAN WELDING SOCIETY)

AXIS:

A real or imaginary line passing through the rotational center of an object.

AXIS OF A WELD:

A line projected longitudinally through a weld, perpendicular to the weld's cross section at its center of gravity.

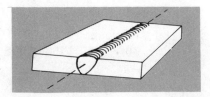

BABBIT:
An alloy consisting of tin, copper, and antimony developed by the American inventor, Isaac Babbit. It has special anti-frictional properties which make it desirable for lining movable machine parts.

BACKFIRE:
Common occurrence during oxy-acetylene welding when flame momentarily withdraws into the torch tip then reappears or is completely extinguished.

BACKHAND WELDING:
A gas welding technique where the torch is held in such a way that the tip points opposite the direction of the weld.

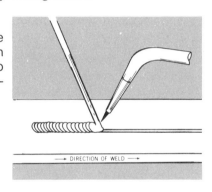

DIRECTION OF WELD

BACKING FILLER METAL:
Filler metal in the form of a ring, strip, or consumable insert, fused into a welded joint with a single pass.

BACKING STRIP:
A light piece or strip of metal used to support or back a weld.

BACKING WELD:
Support or backing in the form of a weld.

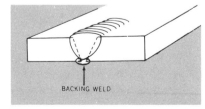

BACKING WELD

BACKSTEP SEQUENCE:
A welding sequence in which a succession of short beads are deposited in a direction opposite to the weld direction.

BALLING UP:
The beads of flux or molten filler metal which form during the brazing process as a result of not having fluxed the base metal sufficiently.

BALL-PEEN HAMMER:
A hammer having a head which is flat at one end and round at the other. Used by machinists and welders for striking chisels and punches on the flat end. The peen or round end is used for riveting. (See: HAMMER)

BAND SAW:
A saw having a blade which forms a continuous loop, mounted on pulleys, used for fast controlled cutting of metals. Better quality models have an adjustable hydraulic feed system and a quick change tension adjustment. Quality models also use a wet cutting system in which coolant is pumped from a reservoir over the blade and recirculated.

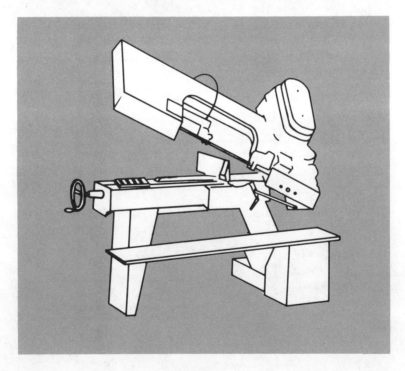

BAR CLAMP:

A work holding device used for securing or positioning extra-long work pieces.

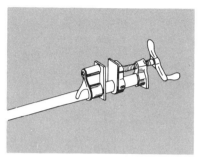

BAR FOLDER:

A machine which folds edges or creases light gage sheet metal. May be used to form square joints and make various angular metal constructions.

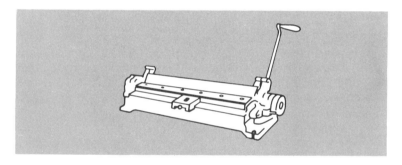

BASE METAL:

The metal which is to be welded, soldered or cut.

BASTARD FILE:

A coarse-cutting file. This common term "bastard" is a corruption of the original designer's name, Barsted. Bastard files may be of either the double cut or single cut variety. These may be either flat, half-round, or full-round in shape. (See: FILE)

BAUXITE:

The principal ore from which aluminum is extracted. Approximately four pounds of this ore will produce one pound of aluminum. (See: ALUMINUM)

BAYONET SAW:

The bayonet saw is a general purpose saw used for cutting wood, plastic, or metal. The metal cutting blade for this saw is made of hacksaw quality stock and may have from 10 to 24 teeth per inch. Extruded aluminum, galvanized sheet metal, pipe, bar stock, and round steel may be handily cut with this portable hand tool. Work to be cut should at all times be firmly clamped in a vise or clamped to a saw horse or table top.

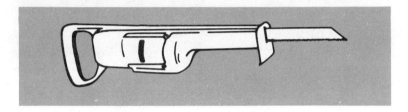

BEAK HORN STAKE:

A shaping tool over which metal is alternately hammered and heated. The hammered metal assumes the form dictated by the convexity or concavity of the horn face. The hornlike stake is inserted into a stable block of hardwood or an anvil for working. (See: STAKE)

BEAM:

A variety of structural steel which is manufactured in three basic designs: the standard H, I and the wide flange. Beams are principally used for weight supporting purposes.

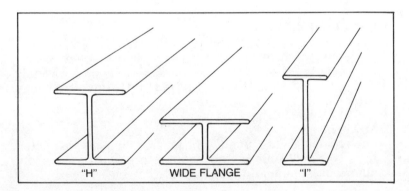

"H"   WIDE FLANGE   "I"

BELLOWS:

An instrument of ancient origin used to create a concentrated blast of air for raising the temperature of a forge fire. Design of this tool has varied greatly through history but generally it consists of a compressible container made of leather and wood. It may or may not be spring-loaded.

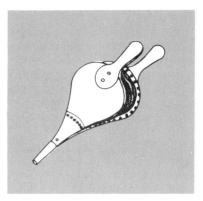

BENCH PLATE:

A type of stakeholding fixture which consists of a flat rectangular steel plate with a variety of square tapered holes of different sizes. The bench plate is fastened to the work bench and the shank of the stake is set firmly in the appropriate square hole while the work is being shaped and formed.

BENCH SHEAR:

A manually operated shear, mounted on a bench, used for cutting light gage metal sheets or strips.

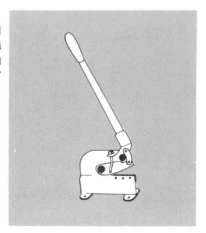

BENCH VISE: (See: VISE, MACHINIST'S)

BENDING JIG (Adjustable):
A tool used for manually bending curved sections of metal. Decorative scrolled curves may be made using this device; a lengthy strip of metal is placed in the jig and manual pressure is applied to start the curve. The metal is moved along as this operation is repeated a number of times until the scroll is completed.

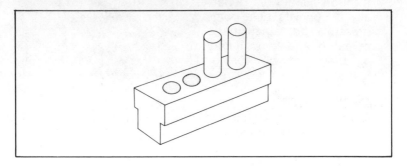

BERYLLIUM:
A strong, yet amazingly lightweight, metal which is used in missiles, aircraft, and in nuclear reactors. This metal weighs approximately eighty percent less than steel, while offering virtually equal strength. It is brittle, but easily machined.

BERYLLIUM BRONZE:
This is an exceptionally strong copper alloy which accrues strength with aging. With between 2 percent and 3 percent beryllium this nonferrous alloy is employed for making non-sparking, safety wrenches for use with oxy-acetylene welding equipment.

BESSEMER STEEL:
A mild, soft steel manufactured by the Bessemer process and used for making girders, rails, boilers, etc.

BEVEL:
An angular edge preparation for welding. Inclination of the angle may be any other than 90°.

BICHROMATE DIPPED FINISH:
This is a finish on copper or brass which gives a color approaching the true color of the metal. It is obtained by the action of a bichromate and sulphuric acid bath which completely removes oxides and scale.

BIDRIWORK:

An ancient decorative metalworking technique which originated in India and is still practiced today. Pure silver in wire and sheet form is inlaid in objects which have been cast of a nonferrous alloy of zinc, copper, and lead. The special quality of this technique depends upon the contrast between the whiteness of silver inlay and the polished blackened alloy background.

BIT:

That part of a soldering iron which actually transfers heat and solder to a joint. (See: SOLDERING IRON)

BLACKSMITH WELDING: (See: FORGE WELDING)

BLACKSMITH'S LEG VISE:

This vise is primarily used for holding work which must be beaten with a heavy hammer.

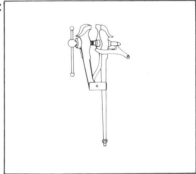

BLACKWORK:

Work done by a blacksmith. The work of a silversmith is called "whitework"

BLANK:

The metal removed from a sheet during a stamping process. As a term in engineering, it is a piece of metal forged, cast, or roughly cut to a desired shape prior to final, close tolerance finishing. In sheet metalworking, it is a shape cut to a certain size preparatory to other operations.

BLANKING:

A stamping operation in which a desired shape is cut from flat sheets or strips of metal using a die.

BLIND JOINT:

Any joint which is hidden from view.

BLOWHOLE:

A casting defect which appears on the surface of a casting in the form of a bubble caused by air or gas having been locked in the mold.

BLOWPIPE:

The welding tool which controls the mixture and flow of gases during oxy-acetylene welding. Historically, blowpipes were little more than mouth-operated metal tubes, which were used to direct a concentrated stream of air or other gases into a flame to intensify the heat.

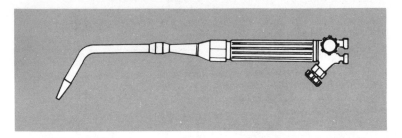

BLOWTORCH:

A burner which operates on benzine or alcohol fuel. The fuel tank is pressurized by a hand pump. The unit performs many of the same functions as a propane torch, such as paint removal, soldering and brazing.

BLUING:

Gun barrels are often "blued." In metalworking this is simply heating metal until it takes on a blue cast.

BOND LINE:

During welding this is the junction where the filler metal and the base metal melt.

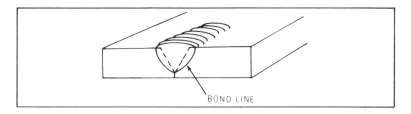

BOND LINE

BORAX:

A crystalline salt (sodium tetraborate) which is the most commonly used soldering flux for a majority of ferrous and nonferrous metals. Borax does not dissolve oxides of aluminum and lead, therefore, other solder and fluxes are required.

BOSS:

A raised shape which appears on the front of metal as a result of its having been worked from behind. The word embossing is derived from this metal technique. Also, a projection, usually cylindrical on a casting.

BOUGING:

A process for correcting surface irregularities in metal which have occurred during raising. The surface to be smoothed is placed over a mushroom or T stake then hammered with a rawhide mallet until a smooth regular surface is achieved.

BOX WRENCH:

This wrench takes its name from the fact that its body completely surrounds or "boxes" a bolt head or nut. It is usually preferred over other wrenches because it will not slip.

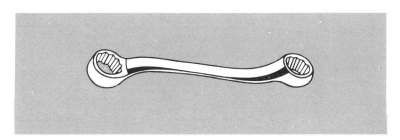

BRAKE (Sheet Metal):

A manually-operated machine for bending and folding light gage metal sheets. It handles larger materials than is possible with the bar folder.

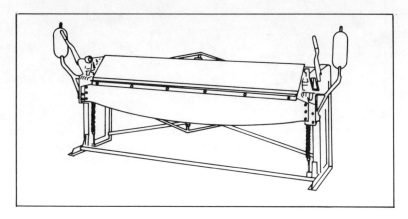

BRASS:

A bright yellow-colored alloy of copper and zinc which lends itself well to fabrication and treatment of every kind. It can be cast, rolled, drawn, embossed, and cut. Brasses which contain more than 36 percent zinc are superior for hot-working. The cold-working qualities of brass alloys containing less than 36 percent zinc are excellent. The very low zinc brasses (5 to 20 percent) are widely used in costume jewelry manufacture. (See PINCHBECK METAL, RED BRASS, MUNTZ BRASS, NAVAL BRASS and CARTRIDGE BRASS)

BRAZING:

A hand soldering technique in which two pieces of metal are heated to a temperature in excess of 430°C (806°F), and are then bonded by the addition of brass or other nonferrous filler metal, and a flux. The process is especially useful for joining dissimilar metals such as copper to steel or brass to wrought iron.

BRINELL HARDNESS TEST:
A method for measuring the hardness of metals. A steel ball one centimeter in diameter is pressed into the smooth surface of a test metal plate for a set amount of time under a given pressure. The diameter of the indentation made by the ball is measured and a comparative hardness is deduced from a Brinell conversion scale. On the Brinell scale metals may range in hardness from about 10 in the case of lead up to 600 or more for heat-treated steels. Dr. Johan A. Brinell of Sweden developed this test around the turn of the century.

BRISTOL WRENCH:
This type wrench or key is L-shaped and made from round stock. One end is fluted to fit the recessed flutes or splines in the Bristol setscrew. Bristol head set and cap screws are not widely used in machine shops and on equipment.

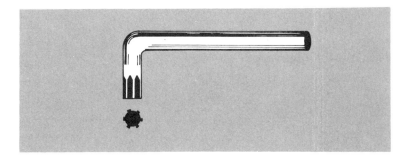

BRITANNIA METAL:
An alloy consisting predominantly of tin and containing no lead. The proportions and contents of the alloy are 91 percent tin, 7 percent antimony and 2 percent copper. The terms britannia metal and pewter are used synonymously by craftsmen though they are two different alloys. The original pewter alloy contained a high percentage of lead and was therefore toxic. Britannia offers several advantages over pewter and none of the drawbacks. Britannia is primarily used today for making decorative articles and for sculptural casting.

BRONZE:

A copper-tin alloy which is reddish-gold and usually darker in color than brass. It is harder than brass and is also more expensive. The tin content ranges from 1.25 to 10 percent in phosphor bronze which is valued for casting uses by sculptor-founders today. Most modern bronzes contain several elements other than copper and tin. Traces of zinc, aluminum, nickel, manganese, silicon, or phosphorus may be found in various alloys of bronze.

BUFFING:

The process of giving metal a lustrous finish. Buffing is most readily accomplished by using machine mounted cloth disc wheels which are charged with a compound such as tripoli, crystalline silica, or Vienna lime.

BUILD-UP SEQUENCE:

The order according to which multiple-pass weld beads are deposited in a joint. The illustration below shows in cross-section a typical ordering of bead deposits in a single-vee groove welded joint.

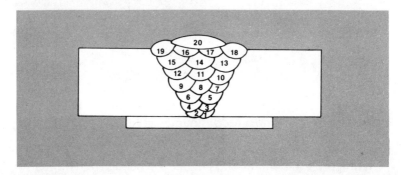

BURIN:

A metal engraving tool sometimes called a "graver." Made from tooled-steel rod, this tool is made in dozens of cross-sectional shapes. It has a mushroom shaped removable or permanent wooden handle.

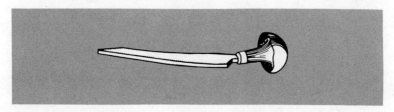

BURNISHING:
A metal-finishing process wherein a surface is mechanically compressed. Work to be finished in this way is often tumbled in a tank with steel balls.

BURNOUT:
During lost wax casting, before molten metal can be poured into the mold the wax pattern must be melted out in a kiln or oven. This process cleans the mold and removes excess moisture from the plaster. (See: LOST WAX CASTING)

BURN-THROUGH:
A welding fault caused when the torch is held for too long in one spot or when too large a welding tip is used.

BURR:
A projecting, sharp edge remaining after cutting, stamping or machining. Burrs are frequently a personal hazard if they are not removed.

BUTT JOINT:
A welded joint which is made when the edges of two pieces to be joined are positioned against each other lying in the same plane. (See: JOINTS, BASIC WELDED)

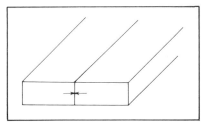

Notes

CALIPER:

A tool predominantly used for measuring inside and outside surface distances. It is made in two basic designs: the inside type and the outside type. The inside caliper measures the diameter of bores, holes and cylinders. The outside caliper measures the outside diameter of circular work.

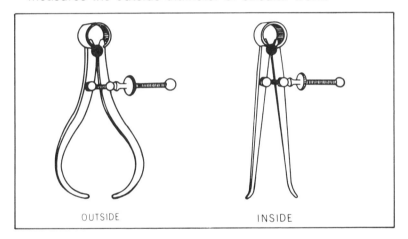

OUTSIDE   INSIDE

CARBIDE:

One or more metallic elements compounded with carbon.

CARBON-ARC WELDING:

An early form of welding patented in 1885 in England by two scientists, N.V. Bernardo and S. Olszewski. This process uses a non-consumable electrode made of carbon or graphite. The welding is done by heating the metal with an arc made between the carbon electrode and the work. The process uses no shielding gas. A filler metal may or may not be used.

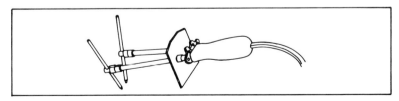

CARBON STEEL: (See: STEEL, CARBON ALLOYS)

CARBORUNDUM:
An abrasive product trade name which is mistakenly used as a generic name for silicon carbide powdered abrasive.

CARBURIZATION:
The introduction of carbon to steel by the addition of carbonaceous material (coke or coal) to steel while it is in a molten state. This process may also be accomplished by heating solid steel below its melting point while it is in contact with carbonaceous materials.

CARBURIZING FLAME: (See: FLAME, CARBURIZING)

CARTRIDGE BRASS:
Sometimes referred to as naval brass or 70:30, or spinning brass, this alloy (70 percent copper; 30 percent zinc) has been used for making shell casings by the military and firearms industry. Also, this alloy has excellent working properties and is used for many spinning and drawing applications.

CASE-HARDENING:
The hardening of steel by heating it to its critical temperature and then submerging it in oil or water.

CASTING:
Any of several processes which involve the pouring of molten metal into a hollow mold in order to form objects. This term also refers to the form or object resulting from the process. (See: SAND MOLD CASTING and LOST WAX CASTING)

CAST IRON:
A ferrous metal alloy made from pig iron. It is the most widely used metal for industrial casting. Cast iron is hard, rigid, wear resistant and it has good machinability. It is also the cheapest metal to produce. It cannot be forged, tempered, or rolled. It has a high carbon content containing between 2.75 and 3.75 percent carbon.

CAUSTIC DIP:
A sodium hydroxide solution in which metal is immersed in order to clean it. Aluminum alloys are dipped so that their macrostructure is revealed.

C-CLAMP:
A C-shaped holding device having an adjustable threaded bolt through one end.

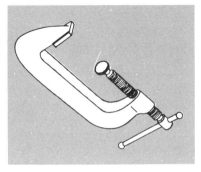

CEMENTED CARBIDES:
A very hard cutting tip made of pulverized carbide steel used in the making of high speed cutting tools.

CENTER GAGE:
A flat metal gage having a 60 degree point and 60 degree V's cut into it for testing the accuracy of lathe centers and for testing and setting up a threading tool prior to chasing threads on a lathe.

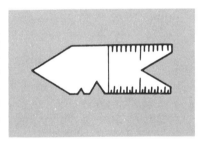

CENTER PUNCH: (See: PUNCH, HAND)

CENTRIFUGAL CASTING:
A casting technique in which the mold is mechanically rotated during pouring and solidifying of the molten metal.

CERMET:
The hardest high speed cutting tip known to man. It is a combination of ceramics and metal which resists breakdown at very high temperatures.

CHAMFERING:
The beveling and finishing of a metal object's edges, usually at a 45 degree angle.

CHANNEL IRON:

A standard structural steel shape which consists of two parallel flanges at right angles to the web. It is manufactured in bar sizes of less than three inches and in structural sizes of three inches and over.

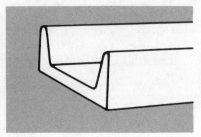

CHASING:

Involves the refined finishing or surface decoration of metal castings. Sheet metal chasing involves punching and hammering which causes plastic variations in the surface.

CHASING HAMMER:

A hammer of unusual conformation, used in metal chasing and repousse work. Its steel head consists of a polished striking face up to 1¼ inches across and a ball or cross peen. The hammer has a springy, ten inch, tapered wood handle terminating in an oval, round, or pistol grip (See: HAMMER).

CHATTER MARKS:

Marks or imperfections on a finished surface left usually as a result of erratic machining and vibration.

CHEEK:

In sand casting, the middle section of a three part flask. (See: FLASK)

CHIPPING HAMMER:

A special tool used for forcibly dislodging or breaking away flux and metal residues from arc welded filler beads. Helps insure a sound weld that is nonporous and free of impurities.

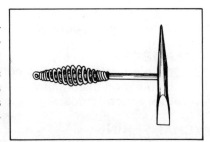

CHISEL:

(See: COLD CHISEL)

CHROME PICKLE:

A means of chemically treating magnesium in a nitric acid, sodium dichromate solution in order to produce a corrosion resistant film on the metal. This film also provides a base for paint.

CHROMIUM:

An alloying element most frequently added to steel to increase hardness. Steel alloys containing more than four percent chromium are called "stainless" because of their special ability to resist corrosion and weathering. (See: STAINLESS STEEL)

CHUCK:

A device most commonly having adjustable jaws for holding drill bits, tools or materials to be worked upon. One chuck which is an exception to the adjustable jaw type is the permanent magnet type. The most commonly encountered varieties of chucks include the Jacob's, 3-Jaw Universal, 4-Jaw Independent, and the draw-in type.

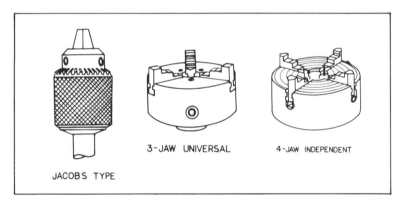

JACOBS TYPE   3-JAW UNIVERSAL   4-JAW INDEPENDENT

CIRE PERDUE:

(See: LOST WAX CASTING)

CLAD BRAZING:

A sheet of metal which has been overlaid with brazing filler metal. Sculptors use brazed overlays to create special color and textural effects on metal.

CLADDING:

An industrial process wherein one metal is covered with another. The cladding metal is applied in a thick layer, then cold rolled through a mill which results in a clad composition.

COALESCENCE:

In welding this term refers to the fusion of two or more separate metal parts through the application of heat and/or pressure.

COATED ELECTRODE:

In arc welding a flux covered filler metal wire which protects the molten metal from the atmosphere during welding. The flux covering is thick and consists of cellulose and/or various minerals. This coating improves welds and stabilizes the arc. Each manufacturer of electrodes develops his own flux coating. The quality of welds depends to a large extent on the welder's knowledge and choice of the right electrode for a particular task.

COIN:

The stamping or forming of a metal piece in a single operation. Stamped work usually has a surface design.

COLD CHISEL:

A cutting tool having a beveled edge. Unlike most other chisels, the cold chisel has no handle; it is an all steel construction, used for cutting, engraving, or mortising metal. A side-cutting chisel is a type of single bevel cold chisel used for cutting the heads off of bolts and rivets.

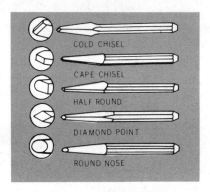

COLD CHISEL
CAPE CHISEL
HALF ROUND
DIAMOND POINT
ROUND NOSE

COLD ROLLING:

A means of slightly reducing the size of hot rolled steel stock after it has cooled. High pressure cold rolling is a means of producing a smooth, brightly finished steel in exact sizes.

COLD SHUT:

In casting, a crack or line of separation which results from the incomplete fusion of two streams of molten metal. This incomplete fusion occurs because one stream of metal has cooled prematurely.

COLLAR:

A means of fastening decorative wrought iron sections. Popularly used during the pre-welding era. A flat length of iron is beveled at the ends to overlap and to be fitted hot. Joining is mechanical rather than welded.

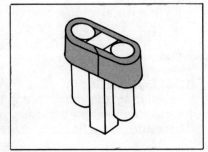

COLOR TEMPERING:

When it is heated, steel changes color. These color changes may be used to determine specific degrees of hardness.

COMBINATION SQUARE SET:

This tool fulfills several functions. It gages depth and height. It may be used to locate the exact center of round stock. Also, it may be adjusted to show virtually any required angle. This set comes equipped with a calibrated blade and three sliding heads which give it multiple usefulness. The square head serves as a height, depth or scribing gage. The V-shaped center head is principally used for locating shaft or round stock center points. The protractor head may be adjusted to indicate any angle from 0-180 degrees both ways.

COMPOSITE JOINT:

A joint which combines a welded and a mechanical joining process.

COMPRESSIVE STRENGTH:

Refers to a metal's ability to be squeezed or compressed without cracking.

CONE:

In oxy-acetylene welding the cone is the wedge shaped part of the flame which is the hottest part and the part nearest the orifice of the torch tip.

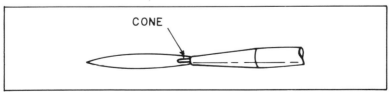

CONE

CONTINUOUS SEQUENCE:
A series of welding passes which are made without interruption from one end of a joint to the other.

CONTINUOUS WELD:
A weld which is unbroken and extends the entire length of a joint. In the case of a circular joint made, for instance, by fusing two sections of steel pipe, the weld extends completely around the joint.

COPE:
In sand casting, the upper half of the flask or frame.

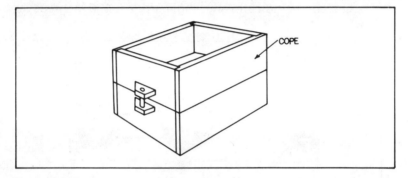

COPPER:
A highly ductile red metal which is extensively used in the arts and in industry. It is used in the composition of bronze and brass alloys. In its pure state craftsmen hammer, anneal and shape copper into a countless variety of functional and artistic forms.

COPPER STEEL:
This is a classification given any steel alloy which specifies a minimum copper content. The addition of copper to steel enhances the metal's corrosion resistance.

CORE:
A mass of material such as sand, plater or clay used to fill the interior cavity of a mold from which a hollow casting is made. When casting is complete the core material is usually removed. Cores may be left intact when access for removal is impossible. The core saves metal, making the casting more economical while decreasing its weight.

CORED SOLDER: (See: ACID CORE SOLDER)

CORNER JOINT:

The two members of this joint are positioned approximately at right angles to each other to form an L. (See: JOINTS, BASIC WELDED)

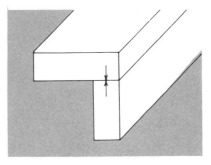

CORROSION:

The destruction of metal through its chemical breakdown into oxides or metallic salts.

CORRUGATED SHEETS:

A variety of black or galvanized steel sheets produced in crimped or wavelike patterns. The corrugations give the sheets structural strength and load carrying capacity. The main use is for exterior roofing and siding.

CORTEN STEEL:

This steel develops a permanent rust brown finish or patina, and has become popular for fabricating large outdoor sculptural monuments. It is somewhat stronger than conventional steel, but may be welded using ordinary steel welding rods.

CORUNDUM:

A commonly used abrasive made of a very tough aluminum oxide. On a one to ten scale of gemmological hardness, corundum rates nine; only diamond is harder.

COUNTER BORE:

To enlarge the diameter and depth of a hole to a specified size.

COUNTERSINKING:

An operation in which a chamfer is cut in a hole to permit a flatheat fastener to be inserted so that the head sets flush with the surface.

COUNTERSINKING TOOL

COUPONS:
These are small pieces of metal used for teaching purposes, demonstrations, and experimental welding.

COVER GLASS:
This glass is the clear outermost piece used in welding goggles, hand shields and helmets. It protects the underlying tinted filter glass from spattered hot flux and metal.

CRITICAL TEMPERATURE:
The temperature at which the internal structure of a metal is altered. For instance, when carbon steels are heated to the critical point they become nonmagnetic. Also, the temperature at which a given alloy of steel may be hardened. This temperature may range from 600°C (1112°F) to 1316°C (2400°F) depending on the carbon and alloying content.

CROCUS CLOTH:
A commercially available metal polishing cloth which is made by adhesively bonding crushed particles of iron oxide to a tough pliable fabric. The particles of iron provide the finely abrasive action which polishes metal.

CROWBAR (Pinch Bar, Wrecking Bar):
A heavy iron or steel bar which measures two to three feet in length, and has one flat or wedge-shaped end. As a metalworking tool, it is typically used as a lever for shifting or moving substantial loads of metal short distances.

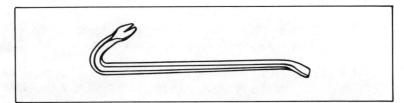

CRUCIBLE:
A receptacle in which metals are melted for most foundry procedures. It is designed to withstand high temperatures and is made of cast iron, cast or wrought steel, clay, graphite, or other refractory material.

CRUCIBLE SHANK:

When it is removed from the melting furnace, the metal-filled crucible is placed in the crucible shank for pouring. This tool is manufactured in either a one-man or two-man crucible handling design.

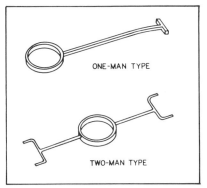

ONE-MAN TYPE

TWO-MAN TYPE

CRUCIBLE TONGS:

An adjustable gripping and carrying device used for removing crucibles filled with molten metal from the melting furnace and transporting them to the pouring site.

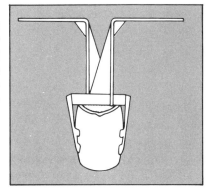

CUPELLATION:

A primitive method of gold and silver refining. Initially, the ore is placed in a shallow, porous cup or cupel, then the cupel is heated to a high temperature and blasted with air. The base metal sinks and is oxidized, the precious metal can then be poured off.

CUTTERS (Milling):

A cutting tool which is used for metal removal in machine shops and manufacturing. Cutters are mounted on arbors, shanks or directly on the spindle nose of milling machines. Cutters come in a wide variety of standard forms and shapes.

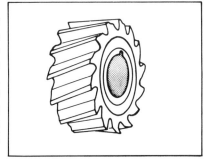

CUTTING ATTACHMENT:

A gas welding torch is converted into a cutting tool by removing the welding tip from the regular torch body and attaching in its place a cutting assembly.

CUTTING, GAS: (See: OXY-ACETYLENE CUTTING)

CUTTING, OXYGEN-VALVE LEVER:

The flow of pure cutting oxygen through the cutting torch is regulated by depressing this device.

CUTTING TIP:

Located always nearest to the work, this part of the cutting torch is where the gases are released into the air.

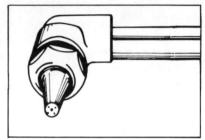

CUTTING TORCH (Oxy-acetylene):

This tool fulfills two functions which are necessary for the successful cutting of metal: (1) It controls and aims the flow of gases used for preheating the metal which is to be cut; (2) It aims the pure oxygen used to cut the metal.

CYANIDING:

A case-hardening process for ferrous alloys during which a metal is heated in molten cyanide. This process is followed by quenching which produces a hard outer case on the metal.

CYLINDER:

A portable bottle-shaped steel container or tank which expedites the safe storage and transportation of compressed welding gases. Cylinders are manufactured in a variety of sizes and shapes.

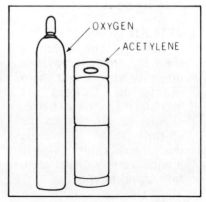

DAMASCENE:

An old Egyptian and Chinese metal decorating process wherein gold or silver wire was inlaid or encrusted into bronze, iron or steel. Today, kuftgari is a modern form of damascene practiced in India and elsewhere. Fourteen to sixteen gage steel is the base metal employed and silver or gold wire is used for inlaying.

DAPPING:

A process of forming and altering small scale pieces of metal using various shaping tools in combination with light hammering.

DAPPING BLOCK:

A square steel block which has a series of hemispherical depressions of many sizes on each of its six sides. For each depression there is a dapping punch of corresponding size. The dapping block and punches are used to form metal hemispheres which may be joined by soldering to form spheres.

DAPPING PUNCH (Dap):

A tool shaft with an almost complete ball at one end. Sets of these punches are used in conjunction with a dapping block and hammer to form metal hemispheres and spheres.

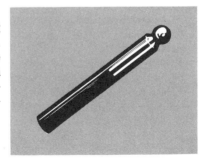

D.C.: (See: DIRECT CURRENT)

D.C. REVERSE POLARITY:
The flow of electrons will be from the work to the electrode when the electric welder is adjusted for direct current-reverse polarity welding. Heat generated during welding is concentrated on the electrode rather than on the work. This means that weld penetration is shallow and electrodes are rapidly consumed. Reverse polarity should be selected for welding light gage metal where burn through is a problem.

D.C. STRAIGHT POLARITY:
When the electric arc welder is adjusted for direct current-straight polarity welding, the flow of electrons will be from the electrode to the work. This means that the heat generated during welding is concentrated on the work rather than on the electrode. Weld penetration is deep into the metal being welded, and the electrode is consumed at a slower rate than is the case with D.C. reverse polarity welding. Straight polarity is especially useful for welding heavy sections of metal.

DEAD-SMOOTH FILE:
A metal finishing file having the finest cutting tooth available. (See: FILE)

DEEP DRAWING:
The shaping and forming of articles by forcing sheet metal into dies and preform molds.

DEPTH OF FUSION:
The strength of a weld depends greatly upon the depth of the fusion in a joint. This may be determined by measuring the distance that fusion extends beneath the original surface of the base metal.

DIAGONAL CUTTING PLIERS:
These pilers are used for cutting small, light material, such as wire and cotter pins. They are designed for cutting only, and the cutting edges are diagonally offset approximately fifteen degrees. They are not suitable for holding work because they exert a greater shearing force than that of other types of similar sized pliers.

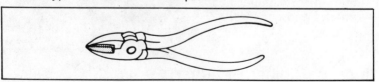

DIE:

A tool used for cutting external screw threads either manually or by machine.

DIE-STAMPING:

The process by means of which holes or openings are cut in sheet metal. This may be done by hand or with the aid of a hand-operated or hydraulic press. (See: PUNCH AND MATRIX)

DIE STOCK:

The handle for holding a threading die.

DIFFUSION PLATING:

A metal plating process which utilizes metallic oxide (metallic powders) which can form an alloy with the base metal may be used in this process.

DIPPING:

The simplest and most direct plating process. It involves simply submerging the metal to be coated in a bath of molten plating metal. Dipping necessitates preliminary surface treatment such as roughening or pickling of the metal to be coated.

DIRECT CURRENT:

An electrical current flowing in one direction only. Alternating current (A.C.) by contrast reverses its direction at regularly recurring intervals. D.C. is the abbreviation for direct current.

DISTORTION:

The heat-related expansion and contraction which alters the configuration of welds and base metal during the welding process.

DIVIDER:

A compass having two steel points. It is used for setting off distances, finding the center point of circles, and scribing or scratching lines in metal surfaces. Measurements may be transferred from rules to metal with the divider.

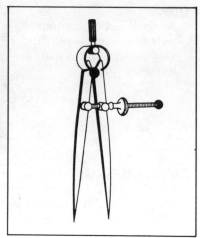

DOUBLE CUT FILE:

This file has two crossing series of cuts which form diamond-shaped teeth. The double cut file generally removes more metal than the single cut, and is used for quick metal removal and rough work. (See: FILE)

DOUBLE END RING CLAMP:

A special hand clamp used for holding rings as they are being worked.

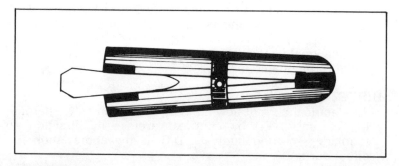

DOVETAIL:

An interlocking joint which allows a forward and backward sliding motion. A typical application in metal is the cross-slide on a lathe.

DRAFT:

The clearance on a casting pattern that permits easy withdrawal of the pattern from the mold.

DRAG:

In sand casting, the lower part of the flask or frame.

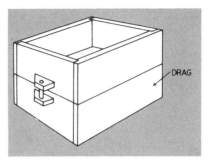

DRAWING:

The stretching and shaping of metal by hammering and heating. Also, the tempering of carbon steels by sub-critical heating and quenching.

DRAWPLATE:

A hardened, high carbon steel plate having a series of conically shaped holes with graduated diameters. Wire is pulled or drawn through these holes to reduce it in size and gage.

DRAWTONGS:

A heavy iron tong designed for use in combination with a drawplate for hand drawing wire. The point of the wire to be reduced or drawn is inserted through a hole in the drawplate; this point is then gripped with the tongs and the wire is manually drawn.

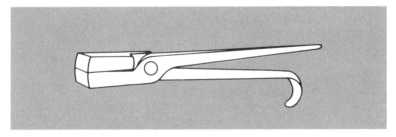

DRIFT:

An obsolete relative of the punch and chisel. Before the advent of power lathes and drills this tool was used by the blacksmith to enlarge, shape and smooth holes in metal.

DRILL CHUCK:

A three jawed clamping device for securely holding the drill bit during the drilling operation. (See: CHUCK, JACOB'S TYPE)

DRILL CHUCK KEY:

A wrench designed especially for tightening or loosening the jaws of the drill chuck.

DRILL GAGE:

A flat steel plate drilled with holes having diameters which correspond to standard drill sizes. Use of this gage can insure selection of the proper size drill.

DRILL PRESS:

A geared, motor-driven, variable speed power tool used primarily for drilling and boring. It is typically mounted on a vertical column affixed to a stationary floor base. An adjustable work holding table is attached to the column. In operation the drive mechanism, including the motor, drill chuck, and bit are lowered onto the work which is held in place on the work table.

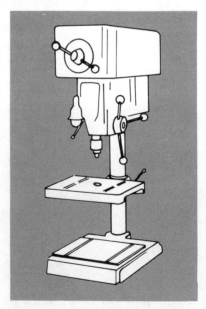

DRILL PRESS VISE:

Used for securely holding small pieces which are to be drilled with a drill press. As a safety precaution the vise should be fastened to the drill press table.

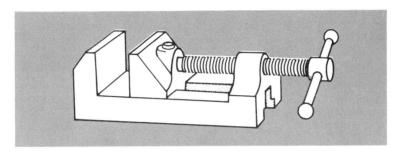

DROP: (See: SPALLING)

DROP FORGING:

A metal forming operation in which a drop hammer falls vertically striking the workpiece between two dies which meet at the bottom of the travel. The top half of the die is mounted in the hammer face while the lower half of the die is mounted in an anvil base.

DROSS:

The metal oxides which form on or in molten metal during welding and casting.

DUCTILITY:

A metal's ability to be drawn into fine wire. There is a relationship between malleability and ductility but not all malleable metals are ductile. Lead is malleable but difficult to draw into wire. Gold is the most highly ductile metal. Other metals in descending order of ductility are silver, platinum, iron, copper, aluminum and nickel.

DUTY CYCLE:

The duty cycle is the amount of time an electric arc welding machine can be operated efficiently at a given amperage. A 40 percent duty cycle rating is adequate for most studio sculptural and craft applications. An arc welder having a 40 percent duty cycle at 180 amps can be operated for 4 minutes out of every 10. As the amperage is adjusted lower on a 40 percent rated welder, the performance factors increase, so that at 100 amps the machine can be operated nine out of every ten minutes.

Notes

EDGE-FLANGE WELD:
When the two pieces of metal constituting an edge point are flanged at the weld location the weld is called "edge-flange."

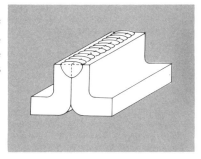

EDGE JOINT:
A joint created where the edges of two or more parallel metal pieces meet. (See: JOINTS, BASIC WELDED)

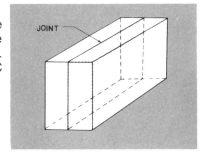

EDGE PREPARATION:
Preliminary to making a sound welded joint, the edges of the metal parts to be joined must be cleaned and modified (shaped) to meet the specifications of the joint to be welded.

ELASTIC LIMIT:
This is the maximum stress which a metal can sustain without showing any signs of permanent stretching after the applied force is released.

ELASTOMERIC ADHESIVES:
These adhesives are made of latex or natural rubber. The addition of sulphur to latex plus heat results in vulcanization and increased bonding strength.

ELECTRODE:

That part of the electric arc welding circuit through which electrical current passes between the arc and electrode holder. Electrodes may or may not be consumed during the welding process. Consumable type electrodes are either bare, composite, covered, emissive, flux-cored, lightly coated or metal. Non-consumable type electrodes are either carbon, tungsten or metal.

ELECTRODE HOLDER:

"Stinger" is the slang term sometimes used to describe this insulated, spring-loaded mechanical device which holds the arc welding electrode and conducts electrical current to it.

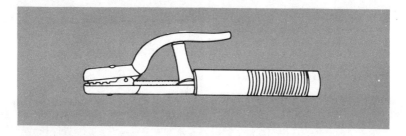

ELECTROMETALLURGY:

A branch of metallurgy which is concerned with the extraction of metal by employing electric current to heat and also to electrolyze ore, treated concentrates or leaching solutions.

ELECTRON BEAM WELDING:

Welding using an electron beam is a newly developed, expensive and often impractical process from the craftsman's point of view. The impracticality of the process stems from the necessity of vacuum-controlled conditions for effective welding operation. Where a vacuum can be established the electron beam process exhibits a pinpoint accuracy which even the laser cannot match.

ELECTROPLATING:

The most widely used method of producing metallic coatings. Electricity is passed through an electrolytic bath containing both the base metal to be coated and the plating metal which is in the form of a dissolved salt. Deposition of the plating metal occurs gradually depending on the current, density, composition, temperature, concentration, and agitation of the bath.

ELECTRUM:
A pale yellow alloy of gold and silver used by the ancient Greeks and Romans.

ENGRAVING:
Engraving in metalwork is the process of incising linear designs with a burin or graver. The process may be done totally by hand, or with the aid of a mechanical device, or completely by machine. Metal engraving originated in Europe during the early Renaissance as a method of decorating armor.

ETCHING:
Creation of designs on metal by blocking out parts of a metallic surface which is to be protected from the action of an acid. Commonly used acid-resisting materials in this process are asphaltum, varnish and beeswax. It was not until the 15th century that European metalworkers began to use etching extensively for decorating armor and weapons.

EXPLOSIVE FORMING:
This is the process of forming metals with explosives. In this technique, a mold, metal and explosives are submerged in a tank of water. A vacuum is created between the metal (preform) and the mold (die). When the explosive charge is released the metal is forced into the mold contour. The distance between the explosive and the metal preform is critical as is the amount of explosive used. Expert engineering has been primarily responsible for making this process useful to industry in recent years for fabricating pieces that are too large to handle using conventional forming methods.

EXTRUSION:
A method of shaping metal into continuous forms (rods and tubes) by forcing it through a die or appropriate configuration.

EZY-OUT:

Bolts and studs which have broken off may be removed from holes with this device. It is manufactured in several sizes and commonly available. To extract a broken screw with this tool, first drill a hole in the screw. The size hole required for each ezy-out is marked on it. The tool is then inserted in the hole, and a counterclockwise turning will remove the broken screw part.

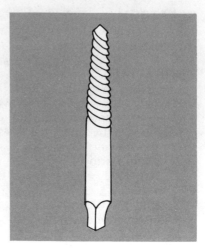

FACE OF WELD:

This is the exposed surface of a weld, the part of the weld metal which is visible to the eye.

FACE PIN SPANNER WRENCH:

This wrench is designed so that it will tighten or loosen a special nut which has holes in its face.

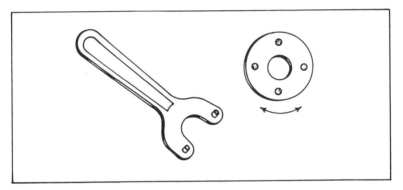

FATIGUE:

The inclination of metal to break or crack under recurring or fluctuating stresses.

FEED:

The rate at which work moves into a mechanical cutting tool to produce a cutting action. Feed may also refer to the movement of a cutting tool into a piece of work. Feed is expressed as inches per minute of cutter metal contact.

FEELER GAGE: (See: THICKNESS (FEELER) GAGE)

FEMALE:

The internal recessed part of any piece of metal into which a screw, bolt or another part fits.

FERRO ALLOY:

A majority of iron-bearing alloys are steels, but these products do not qualify as steel because of the disportionately high amount of alloying elements they contain. These alloys are chiefly used as additives to molten steel. Several of the most common ferro alloys are ferrochromium, ferromanganese, ferrophosphorus, ferrosilicon, and ferrovanadium.

FERROUS METAL:

Any metal alloy which has iron as its primary ingredient.

FILE:

A hardened steel hand tool having sharp cutting ridges or teeth which are used for shaping or smoothing metal and other surfaces such as wood and stone. Files are graded according to the degree of fineness, and according to whether they have single-or- double-cut teeth. (See: DEAD SMOOTH FILE, DOUBLE CUT FILE, or SINGLE CUT FILE)

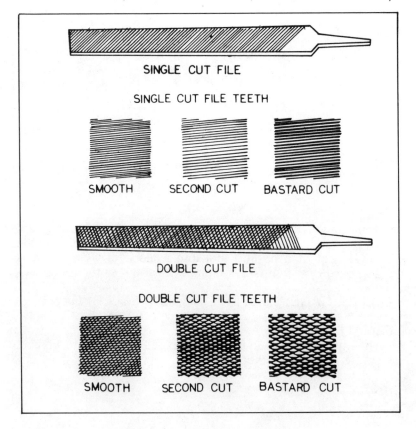

SINGLE CUT FILE

SINGLE CUT FILE TEETH

SMOOTH   SECOND CUT   BASTARD CUT

DOUBLE CUT FILE

DOUBLE CUT FILE TEETH

SMOOTH   SECOND CUT   BASTARD CUT

FILE CARD:

When a file becomes filled or clogged with chips of metal this tool is used for cleaning the clogged teeth.

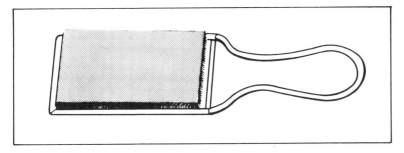

FILIGREE:

A wireworking technique wherein wire is woven, twisted, or wound into decorative shapes or patterns then soldered onto a base metal surface.

FILING VISE:

This portable hand-held device is useful for clamping and holding small work which requires intricate filing and finishing. The work is held between the vice's two jaws which are tightened or loosened by turning a wing nut.

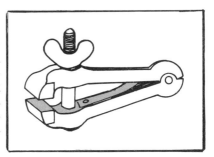

FILLER METAL:

The additional metal needed when welded, brazed or soldered joints are being made. While filler metal is typically used in making welded joints it is not necessary in every situation.

FILLET WELD:

A triangular-shaped weld that joins two metal surfaces which intersect at right angles making a Lap, Tee, or Corner Joint. (See: JOINTS, BASIC WELDED)

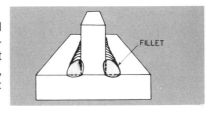

FILLET

FIN:

An irregular thin ridge or projection of metal which remains on a cast piece when it is removed from the mold. This may be caused by a crack in the mold or imperfect joining of the mold parts. Fins are removed by chasing or filing.

FIRE BLANKET:

In the event that a worker's clothes catch on fire, this chemically treated blanket may be safely used to extinguish the flames by quickly wrapping the victim. Fire blankets should be mounted on the wall of welding and foundry areas in metal containers.

FIRESCALE:

A surface oxide which forms on metal as a result of heating, annealing, soldering or welding.

FIT (Screw):

The type and closeness of contact between a screw and threaded parts. Fit may range from loose to wrench tight. A wrench fit requires the use of some tools to tighten the screw, because of a degree of metal interference. A loose fit allows for finger-assembly with ease and speed.

FIXTURE:

A device for holding work in a machine tool.

FLAME, CARBURIZING:

A gas welding flame having an excess of acetylene. This flame is characterized by an intermediate acetylene feather located between the small inner white cone and the outer blue envelope. A carburizing flame adds carbon to the metal, and in reasonable amounts this may increase the tensile strength of welds.

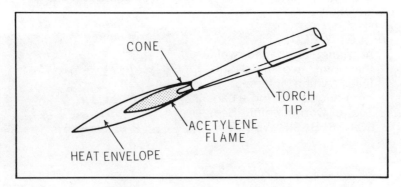

FLAME-HARDENING:

Steel may be made considerably harder and more wear resistant than usual by heating it with the flame of an oxy-acetylene torch, then quenching it in air, water, brine or oil.

FLAME, NEUTRAL:

Gas welding of mild, low-carbon steels and cast iron is done with a flame which has no excess of oxygen or acetylene; in other words, the flame is neither oxidizing nor carburizing. A neutral or normal welding flame is composed of a one-to-one combination of oxygen and acetylene. In appearance the neutral flame shows no feather beyond the inner white cone. It is used for welding low carbon steels and cast iron; and for most brazing operations.

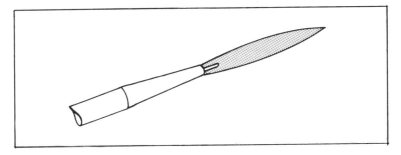

FLAME, OXIDIZING:

A 6300 degree F. flame which results from the introduction of excessive oxygen into the neutral (1 to 1) oxy-acetylene flame mixture. The oxidizing flame has fewer practical applications than other welding flames. It is mainly used for welding brass and bronze. An oxidizing flame may be handy also for brazing galvanized iron. Excessive oxygen in the gas mixture reduces the size of the inner cone of flame and the burning is accompanied by a roaring or hissing noise.

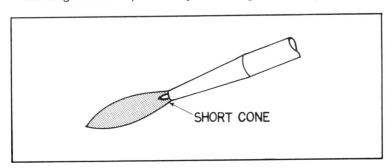

SHORT CONE

FLAME POWDER CUTTING:

This is a comparatively little known and expensive flame cutting procedure. A stream of metallic powder is directed into the cutting zone under air pressure. The powder fluxes the metal oxides in the cut. Cutting is made possible by the lowered melting temperature of the oxide mixture which results from the fluxing action of the powder. This process is well adapted for clean, precision cutting of thick sections of nonferrous metals.

FLASHBACK:

During oxy-acetylene welding it is not uncommon for the flame to suddenly recede into the torch tip, disappearing from view. This occurrence is frequently accompanied by the emission of a hissing and squeaking sound from the torch. The welder must momentarily turn off gas to the torch then reignite the flame using his striker.

FLASK:

In foundry work a wooden or metal frame which holds the sand that forms the mold.

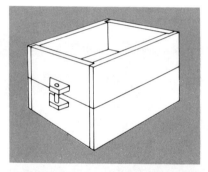

FLAT POSITION:

This is a basic welding position in which the joint and the weld face lie on a horizontal plane at approximately a 180 degree angle.

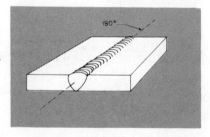

FLORENTINE TEXTURE:

A decorative finish produced by the use of grooved lining tools on metal. This engraving treatment involves the covering of an entire surface with very fine, parallel or cross-hatched lines.

FLUORESCENT PENETRANT INSPECTION:

A nondestructive chemical means for discovering cracks and flaws in welded joints and metals. An oil based penetrant is sprayed onto the surface to be tested; the surface is then rinsed with a solvent to remove excess penetrant; and finally the surface is inspected under a "black light." Defects glow with luminescent clarity.

FLUX (Soldering):

Four basic types of flux are used for soldering. These are: (1) Inorganic — corrosive chemical fluxes consisting of zinc chloride or ammonium chloride dissoved in water. Used mainly for non-electrical applications; (2) Organic — moderately corrosive acids such as glutanic or stearic dissolved in water or alcohol; (3) Rosin — Non-corrosive flux produced from the pine tree. Excellent for electrical soldering; (4) Activated Rosin — A pure rosin flux containing small amounts of strong activating agents which make them almost as active as acid type fluxes minus the corrosive disadvantages.

FLUX (Welding):

Promotes fusing of metals by assisting with the removal of potentially harmful oxides during welding. The addition of a fluxing agent prevents and eliminates many harmful impurities which can weaken welds. Borax is a commonly used flux when forge welding higher carbon steels, while fine silica sand can be used as a flux on low carbon steels.

FLUX-CORED ARC WELDING:

This is one of the newer shielded arc welding processes. Unlike TIG welding this process uses a consumable electrode, and is usually shielded by CO_2 gas. The process gets its name from the fact that the electrode wire used has a flux center, that is, the inside of the electrode wire is filled with flux. This process is primarily production oriented; the electrode wire is automatically and continuously fed into the arc from reels which typically carry fifty pounds of coiled wire.

FORCE FIT:

A permanent fitting of metal parts which is achieved when the interference between two mated parts is such that the use of force is required to press the pieces together. (See: FIT [Screw]).

FOREHAND WELDING:

An oxy-acetylene welding technique wherein the torch tip is pointed in the direction of the weld progress. The torch is tilted about 15 degrees in forehand welding; and smaller torch tips are generally used than is the case when a backhand technique is used. (See: BACKHAND WELDING)

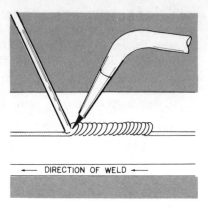

DIRECTION OF WELD

FORGE:

Has two meanings: (A) a furnace or shop where metal is heated and worked, or (B) to forge, that is to form metal by heating, hammering, or pressing.

FORGE WELDING:

Sometimes referred to as blacksmith welding or hammer welding, this process dates from ancient times. Coalescence or fusion is brought about during this process when two pieces of preheated metal in a white hot state are hammered or pressed together, until a firm union is made.

FOUNDRY SAND:

A specially treated mixture of silica and clay used for sand casting. It does not dry out, and may be used repeatedly. Its fineness is carefully controlled so that it will produce accurate, sharp and detailed castings.

FREEZE:

When molten metal cools it changes from a liquid to a solid state, this solidification is called freezing. Water, in a similar way, freezes when it is cooled below 32°F.

FRICTION LIGHTER:

The safest recommended tool for igniting the oxy-acetylene torch is a spark-type friction lighter. A single spark is usually all that is necessary to light the gas torch. Sparks are produced with this tool by simply squeezing the handles together and drawing flint across a ridged steel striker plate.

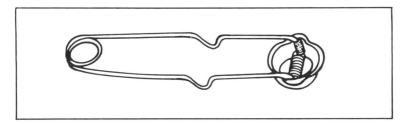

FULLER:

A forging hammer which may be used for making depressions or grooves in hot metal. This hammer is also useful for spreading, fluting, drawing down, and necking hot metal. (See: HAMMER)

FUSION:

The melting together of metals which occurs during welding. This union is a structural as well as a chemical one. (See: COALESCENCE)

FUSION ZONE:

This is a welding term that refers to the area of the base metal that is melted. A cross-sectional view of a weld may be used to determine the exact parameters of this area.

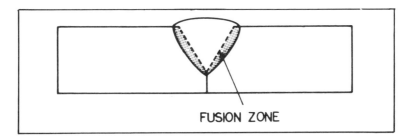

FUSION ZONE

Notes

GAGE:

In the broadest sense, a gage may be any tool or device used for checking metal parts against specified size limitations.

GALVANIZED IRON:

Iron, usually in sheets, which has been coated by a galvanizing process. Galvanizing is a process wherein iron is first pickled in a diluted acid to clean its surface then dipped in molten zinc.

GANGUE:

The extraneous, unwanted materials which usually contaminate ore. Some of these materials are limestone, sand, clay and stone. Various ores are comparatively free of impurities while others like copper may have only one percent metal.

GAR-ALLOY:

This alloy of zinc, copper and silver is used as a pewter substitute, because it is less costly and has several of the qualities of pewter. It is blue gray in color, works well cold, and can be buffed to a high polish. Gar-alloy tarnishes easily and must have a protective coat of lacquer.

GAS METAL-ARC WELDING (MIG):

MIG welding is done by heating metal sections with a gas shielded arc formed between a continuous, consumable, filler metal electrode and the work surface. The major difference between gas metal-arc welding (MIG) and gas tungsten-arc welding (TIG) is that with MIG welding the electrode is consumed. MIG welding units use a consumable electrode in the form of a wire-feed system. The MIG process is used for most types of welding, plus it may be comfortably used for joining aluminum plate thicker than 3.2mm (⅛ in).

GAS TUNGSTEN-ARC WELDING (TIG):

This welding process is most widely used for joining aluminum sections varying in thickness from .8 to 3.2mm ($^1/_{30}$ to $^1/_8$ in). The TIG process is also useful for welding copper and copper alloys, magnesium, stainless steel, silicon bronze, titanium, carbon and low alloy steels. TIG welding is done by heating metal sections with a gas shielded arc formed between a nonconsumable zirconium tungsten electrode and the work. The usual shielding gas for TIG welding is either argon or helium. Filler metal may or may not be used during TIG welding.

GATE:

The point at which poured molten metal enters the mold cavity.

GAUGE: (See: GAGE)

GERMAN SILVER:

A silver substitute used in the manufacture of costume jewelry. It is a copper-based alloy with varying amounts of nickel and zinc. This alloy with a composition of 64 percent copper, 18 percent zinc, is typically used as the base for most silver-plated ware. Its working characteristics are poor in that it is brittle and cannot be hammered into shape.

GLOVES:

Gauntlet-type leather or asbestos gloves provide the best protection from burns which may occur during welding, brazing or soldering. These gloves remain durable for a long while if they are kept free of oil or grease.

GOGGLES:

(Welding and Cutting):
The intense light, heat and flying particles produced during welding, brazing, or oxygen cutting are potential sight hazards. Special tinted optical glass lenses are made for protecting the worker's eyes and reducing the effects of glare. Also, these lenses permit the welder to see his work clearly.

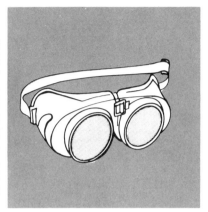

GRANULATION:

A decorative technique for joining minute grains of gold to a base metal and to each other using solder or a chemical reaction. The process was probably originated by the ancient Etruscans who were masters of the technique.

GRAVER: (See: BURIN).

GRINDER:

A bench-mounted or portable machine used for the purpose of abrasive finishing of metal. The principle abrasives which are hard enough for metal grinding are aluminum oxide and silicon carbide.

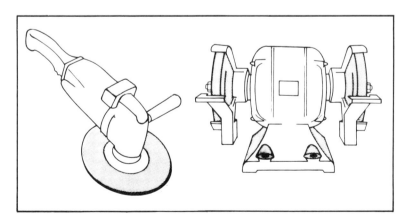

GROOVE WELD:

A weld made in the groove or channel between two metal pieces to be joined. Groove weld types have been generally standardized as follows:

Square	Double-Vee
Single-Vee	Double-Bevel
Single-Bevel	Double-U
Single-U	Double-J
Single-J	Double-Flare-Bevel
Single-Flare-Bevel	Double-Flare-Vee
Single-Flare-Vee	(See: JOINTS, BASIC WELDED)

GROUND CLAMP:

A spring-loaded fastening device which is connected to the loose end of an electric arc welding machine's ground lead cable. During use this device is attached to the metal which is to be welded and forms part of the electrical arc welding circuit.

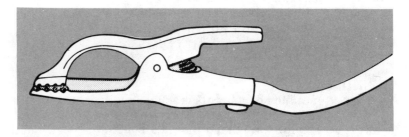

GUIDED-BEND TEST:

A test which indicates the soundness, strength and flexibility of a welded joint. A welded section to be tested is first machined so that the weld is flush with the plate. The test sample should be small enough so that it can be bent in a vise. The bend is started at the welded joint. As the bend becomes more acute, the sample is checked for cracks. If the sample can be bent double without any cracks appearing, the weld is considered sound.

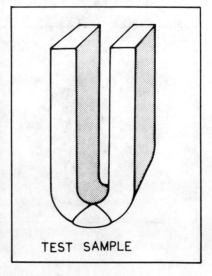

TEST SAMPLE

HACKSAW:

The hacksaw is a metal cutting tool which is most effectively used for cutting light sections of mild steel. The saw frame is adjustable and in appearance resembles an elongated U. The hacksaw blade is typically one-half inch wide, straight and fine-toothed.

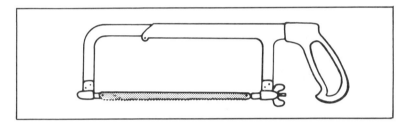

HALF-ROUND FILE:

This is a general-purpose file which has one curved side and one flat side. The curved side is only slightly rounded; it never equals a semi-circle. The rounded side is used for finishing curved surfaces and the flat face is used on flat surfaces.

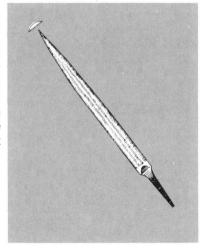

HALLMARK:

A mark or stamp appearing on articles made of precious metals. This stamp signifies the quality of the article, indicates who the maker is, and sometimes shows the date when the piece was assayed and marked.

HAMMER:

A hand tool used for driving, beating, and shaping metal by repeated blows. Hammers generally have hardwood, fiberglass or steel handles with a striking head mounted at one end. An impressive assortment of hammers are available to the metalworker. The weight and shape of the head and striking face vary according to the hammer's intended function.

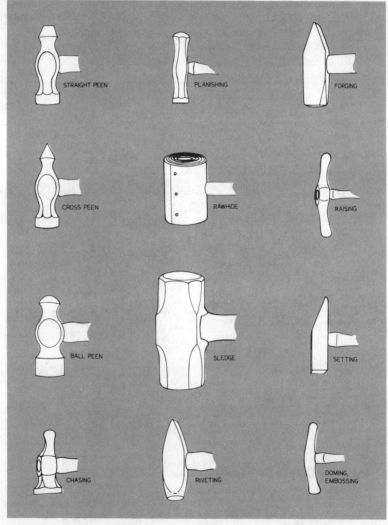

HAMMER WELDING: (See: FORGE WELDING)

HAND GROOVER:

This sheet metal fabricating tool is used to offset outside grooved seams or joints. Hand groovers which are 1.6mm (1/16 in) wider than the width of the finished lock or seam must be used to insure correct offsetting. (See: JOINTS, COMMON SHEET METAL)

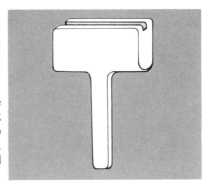

HAND ROLLING MILL:

This manually-operated device is used to reduce the thickness or gage of sheet metal or wire. The mill rolls may be completely smooth or they may be grooved in graduated widths for reducing wire.

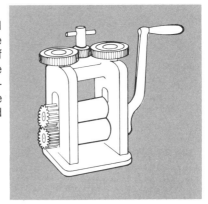

HAND SHIELD:

The hand shield is an arc welding helmet with a hand grip attached. It is especially useful for teaching, because it offers quick and easy eye, face, and neck protection. It is an excellent tool to use for short bead runs and close observation and demonstration.

HARDENABILITY:

The property of ferrous metal alloys which determines the depth and extent of hardness induced by quenching.

HARD HAT:

A protective helmet which is manufactured in a variety of styles. Most hard hats are made of polyethlene or polycarbonate, materials which are ranked among the toughest of head gear synthetics yet developed. These hats are equipped with a shock-absorbing suspension system that offers protection from electrical shock and from accidental head contacts.

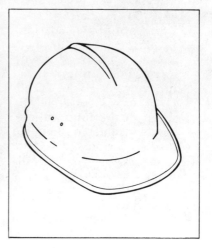

HARDNESS:

A measurable quality of metals, usually calculated by one of three methods: (1) Resistance to indentation (See: ROCKWELL HARDNESS TEST), (2) Stiffness or temper of wrought materials, (3) Ease or difficulty of machining.

HARDNESS TESTS: (See: BRINELL, MOHS, ROCKWELL).

HARD SOLDERING:

A metal joining process which falls somewhere between brazing and soft soldering. Like brazing, hard soldering employs flame heat; and joint design is the same as with soft soldering. A common hard soldering alloy consists of 45-50% silver, 30-35% copper and 15-25% zinc.

HARD SURFACING:

The building up or toughening of metal surfaces by the deposition of welded filler metal. This process is useful for restoring metal parts which have become worn through abrasion, corrosion, or impact.

HARDY:

A wedge-shaped anvil tool which is indispensable for cutting and splitting hot iron and steel. This tool fits snugly into the anvil's square hardy hole and is used as a stationary chisel. Hot metal is placed on the tool's edge, hammered, and rotated until it breaks off.

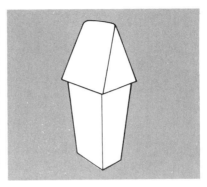

HARDY HOLE:

A 2.5 - 3.7 cm (1-1½ in) square hole in the face of an anvil into which the shank of the hardy is set. (See: ANVIL)

HELMET (Welding):

This indispensable part of the arc welder's protective equipment shields the face, eyes and neck from flying particles, and harmful ultraviolet and infrared rays. Welding helmets are constructed of lightweight, heat-resistant materials. The better quality helmets come equipped with an inner head band which can be attached to a hard hat for increased protection.

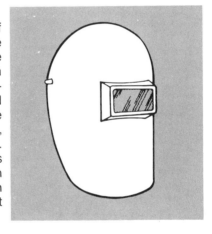

HIGH ENERGY FORMING:

Any metal forming process involving the release of a high energy source such as explosives, electricity, or pneumatic-mechanical. (See: EXPLOSIVE FORMING)

HIGH-SPEED STEEL:

A steel alloy which is used for making metal cutting tools such as taps, cold chisels, machinist's cutters and drills. This alloy is designated "high-speed" because it shows little wear even when it is used under the stress of great pressure and high machining speeds. A typical high-speed steel alloy contains about .7 percent carbon, 18 percent tungsten, and 4 to 6 percent chromium.

HOLDING FURNACE:

A small auxiliary furnace used for maintaining molten metal at the correct casting temperature for a period of time after it has been transferred from a larger melting furnace.

HOOK SPANNER WRENCH:

Many special nuts are made with notches cut into their outer edge. In order to loosen or tighten these notched nuts a uniquely designed wrench is required. It has a curved arm with a hook on the end which fits into one of the notches of the nut.

HORIZONTAL POSITION:

When welding in horizontal position, the axis of the weld lies at an angle of approximately 180 degrees, and the weld face is more or less vertical.

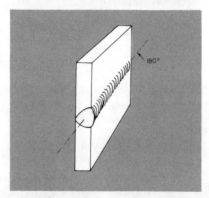

HORIZONTAL ROLLED POSITION:

This term refers to a pipe welding technique wherein welding is done in the flat position by rotating the pipe as the weld is made.

HOSE (Welding):
This hose is a specially made high-strength variety which conveys gases from the welding regulators to the torch. Welding hose is made from reinforced synthetic or natural rubber compounds which are oil and flame resistant. Oxy-acetylene hoses are color coded; the oxygen hose is green and the acetylene hose is red.

HOT ROLLING:
Steel is industrially produced in the form of huge blocks and ingots. While they are hot these ingots are mechanically conveyed through a series of heavy, steel pressure rollers. These rollers compress the hot steel in much the same way that the old style clothes wringers were used to squeeze wet clothes. In this manner hot rolled steel plate, round, and flat stock are produced. Sheet steel of less than 4.8 mm (3/16 in) thickness is produced usually by a cold rolling process.

HOT SHORTNESS:
Hot metal brittleness.

HYDROMETALLURGY:
A branch of metallurgy which is concerned with the removal of metals from ores by treatment with various aqueous acid or chemical solutions. (See: LEACHING)

Notes

INDEPENDENT CHUCK: (See: CHUCK)

INDIA OILSTONE:

An artificial whetting stone made from an aluminum oxide abrasive. This stone comes from the manufacturer impregnated with oil and requires little additional oil during sharpening or honing. These stones are available in three degrees of coarseness: fine for polishing, medium and coarse for cutting.

INERT GAS:

A gas which under normal welding conditions does not chemically combine with either the filler metal or the base metal. Argon and helium are the most common inert gases used in welding.

INGOT:

A cast form, usually poured in an open mold, which is used for remelting.

INLAY:

Any decorative process wherein grooves or areas are cut in a metal surface and another metal is forced into the recessed or hollowed area. Metal-inlay is exemplified by damascene, bidri, and kuftgari work. The term also applies to the inlay of other materials into metal or the inlay of metal into nonmetallic materials like wood, plastic, nylon or shell.

INTERMITTENT WELD:

A weld that is broken at more or less regular intervals over the full length of the joint.

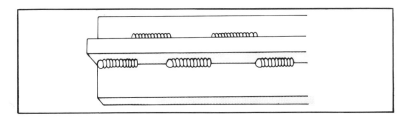

INVAR:

This alloy consists of 36 percent nickel, 63 percent iron and 1 percent of small amounts of manganese, silicon and carbon. Invar has an almost zero rate of thermal expansion at ordinary temperatures. Its invariability makes this alloy useful for pendulums and balances in clocks and automobile pistons.

INVESTMENT CASTING:

A process that involves making a wax, plastic, or even a frozen mercury pattern, enclosing it with a wet refractory material, melting the pattern once the investment has dried and set, and finally pouring molten metal into the cavity. (See: LOST WAX CASTING)

IRON ORE:

The rock forms and aggregates in which iron and other elements are found. There are four main types of ore: (1) hematite — which has as much as 70 percent iron and is reddish-brown in color, (2) magnetite — a sulphur free black stone containing 60 to 70 percent iron. Found mainly in Sweden, (3) limonite — a yellowish-brown rock having from 30 to 50 percent iron and as much as 1 percent phosphorus.

JACOB'S CHUCK: (See: CHUCK)

JEWELER'S SAW:

This saw consists of a spring steel frame which is designed to hold a fine cutting blade. It is used to saw soft, nonferrous metals, however, very thin ferrous metals may be cut also. The frame may be adjustable or non-adjustable. Adjustable frames may have a depth which varies from four to eight inches.

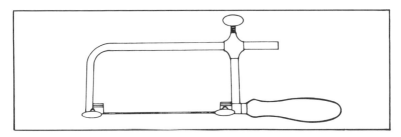

JIG:

A mechanical fixture for locating or holding metal in a desired position. During operations such as drilling or countersinking a jig may be used to guide the cutting tool.

JOINTS, BASIC WELDED:

Following are illustrations of sixteen of the most commonly used fusion welded metal joints. The conditions under which each joint should be used are described. Also, the proper orientation of metal pieces, edge preparation, and weld penetration are indicated.

Plain Butt Joint: Mainly used on plate up to .95 cm ($^3/_8$ in) thick. It is suitable for most normal load conditions.

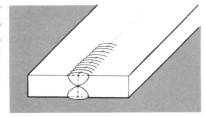

Single-V Butt Joint: A suitable joint for .95 cm ($^3/_8$ in) plate or thicker. It meets all typical load conditions but is costly, requiring more weld metal than the Plain Butt Joint.

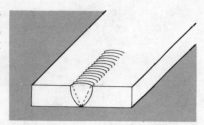

Double-V Butt Joint: A joint which is welded from both sides, and is used largely for 1.2 cm ($^1/_2$ in), or heavier plate. It requires less weld metal than the Single V Joint, but costs more in machining time. It bears all usual loads well.

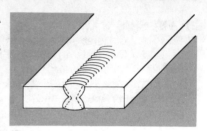

Single-U Butt Joint: When first quality work is required in 1.2 cm ($^1/_2$ in) plate or heavier metal this joint design is used. It costs more to machine than the Single V but requires less filler metal. It is welded from one side, except for a single final weld bead which is run on the opposite side of the joint. This joint meets all usual load conditions.

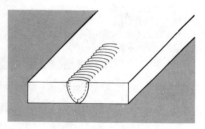

Double-U Butt Joint: Used in plate heavier than 1.2 cm ($^1/_2$ in) where welds can be made from both sides. Also used where savings in filler metal justify an increased machining cost.

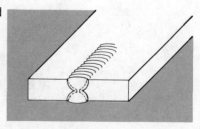

Plain-Fillet, Welded-Tee Joint: Appropriate for all ordinary plate sizes, and used without machining.

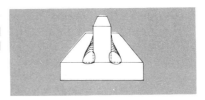

Single-V Tee Joint: For use in plate lighter than 1.2 cm (½ in). It is welded from one side only, and may be more severely loaded than the Flush Corner Joint. Joint preparation is more expensive, but less filler metal is required than with the Flush Corner Joint.

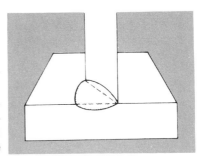

Double-V Tee Joint: Used for heavy plates which are to be welded from both sides. It requires less filler metal than the Flush Corner Joint, and may be used where there are severe longitudinal or transverse stresses.

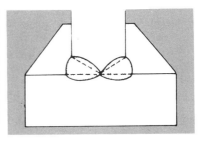

Single-U Tee Joint: This joint is welded from one side only and is recommended for 2.5 cm (1 in) or heavier plates. It is advisable to run a final weld bead on the side away from the U. Machining is more expensive but less filler metal is used than with the Single V joint. Handles load conditions which are the same as for the Half Open Corner Joint.

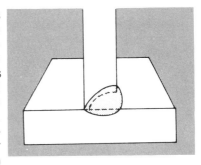

Double-U Tee Joint: For 1.2 cm (½ in) or heavier plate which can be welded from both sides. This joint handles all regular, and most severe load conditions. Joint preparation is costly; but less filler metal is required than with Full Open Corner Joints.

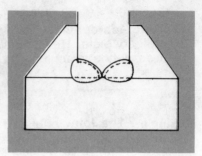

Singel-Bead Lap Joint: May be appropriately used for all sizes of sheet metal and plate when joints are not subject to excessive fatigue or high impact.

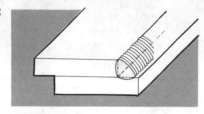

Double-Bead Lap Joint: This joint is better than the Single Bead design and may be used for load conditions which are too severe for a Single Bead Lap Joint. Butt joints are best for use under severe conditions, but are more expensive to produce than Lap Joints.

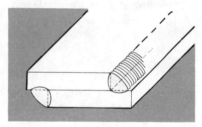

Flush-Corner Joint: Generally used for 12 gage or lighter metal. This joint may be used for joining heavier gage sheets or plate when the load requirements are light.

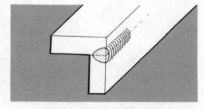

Half-Open, Corner-Joint: Used generally for 12 gage or heavier metal. The weld is made from one side only for ordinary loads, but used with caution for fatigue or impact loads.

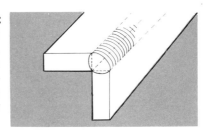

Full-Open, Corner-Joints: Used for all plate thicknesses where the joint is to be subjected to severe load conditions. Provides maximum strength and is welded from both sides.

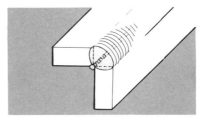

Edge-Joint: This is a joint design recommended for light work and non-severe loads. It is usually employed for .8cm (¼ in) or thinner metal.

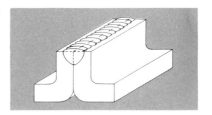

JOINTS, COMMON SHEET METAL:

Light gage sheet metal sections are joined using a wide variety of folded seams. These seams may be made with difficulty by hand or with ease using a bar folder or brake. The joints are typically finished by soldering, riveting or a combination of both. Illustrated below are eleven of the most frequently encountered joints used in sheet metal fabrication.

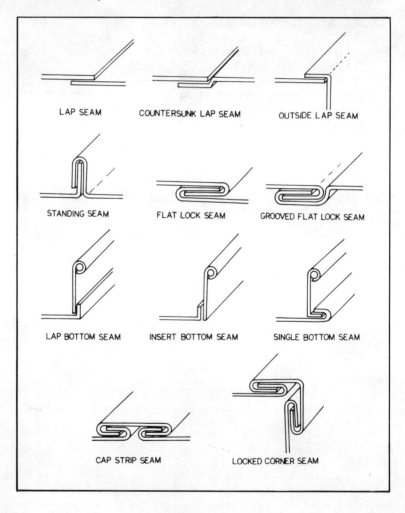

LAP SEAM

COUNTERSUNK LAP SEAM

OUTSIDE LAP SEAM

STANDING SEAM

FLAT LOCK SEAM

GROOVED FLAT LOCK SEAM

LAP BOTTOM SEAM

INSERT BOTTOM SEAM

SINGLE BOTTOM SEAM

CAP STRIP SEAM

LOCKED CORNER SEAM

KERF:
The slit or opening remaining after metal has been displaced by a cutting process.

KEY:
A small piece of metal partially imbedded in a shaft and partially in a hub to lock in place a gear or pulley on a shaft.

KEYWAY:
The slot or recess in a shaft that holds the key. (See: Illustration).

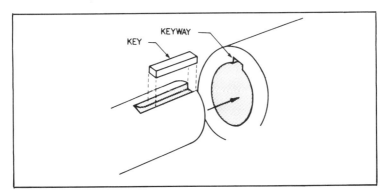

KNURLS:
Rows of uniformly spaced serrations on tool handles which provide a better grip. Knurling is also used by craftsmen for textural decoration.

KUFTGARI: (See: DAMASCENE)

Notes

LADLE:

A vessel used for removing and conveying molten metal from a furnace to molds. This foundry tool may vary in size from a hand-operated version to huge industrial types weighing 100 tons or more.

LAP JOINT:

A welded joint made between two pieces of metal which overlap. (See: JOINTS, BASIC WELDED)

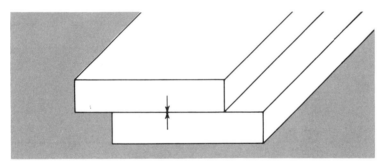

LAPPING:

An abrasive finishing process in which extremely fine abrasives such as diamond dust or various abrasive flours are used.

LASER BEAM WELDING:

A by-product of the development of laser technology, this welding process utilizes coherent light energy from the laser beam to weld hard to fuse, paper thin and thinner materials. The welding of gold, silver and copper is easily handled by this process.

LATHE, METAL TURNING:

A machine in which metal stock is held and rotated as it is being shaped by a cutting tool that is held against the work. Metalworking lathes are generally used for turning, facing, reaming, threading and drilling operations. Lathes vary in size from the microtype used by jewelers to sizes large enough to turn huge rolling cylinders used in the manufacture of steel.

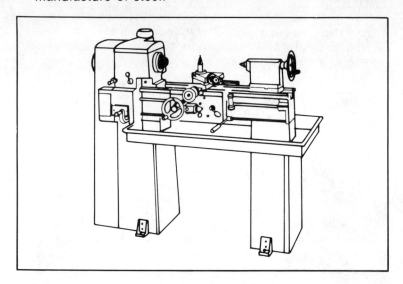

LAY OUT:

To locate and mark or scribe points for machining, forming, and construction operations.

LEACHING:

A chemical process in which liquid solutions of acids, water, ammonia, or sodium cyanide are used to dissolve metals from ores. Copper, manganese, zinc, silver, and gold are separated from ore by this process. (See: HYDROMETALLURGY)

LINEMEN'S PLIERS: (See: SIDE-CUTTING PLIERS)

LINING TOOL (Liner):

A multiple-grooved engraving tool used to create patterns of parallel lines on metal. This tool may be used to score the face of metal to provide a better gripping surface for enamel or niello.

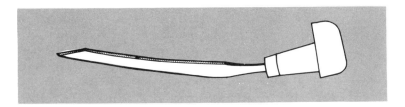

LIQUIDUS:

The flow point of a metal during heating, this is the temperature at which a metal becomes completely liquid.

LIVER OF SULPHUR:

A mixture of potassium sulphides which in combination with water is used to create a patina, or color, on metal surfaces. Metal may be dipped in this solution or it may be wiped or brushed on.

LOAM:

A strongly bonded mixture of clay and coarse sand used for making sand casting molds.

LOST WAX CASTING:

A very precise and ancient way of casting metals that involves making a pattern in wax, investing the pattern or model in a plaster or clay mold. When the mold has dried, a cavity is created by melting out the wax. Molten metal is poured into the cavity and the pattern is reproduced in permanent form.

LUTO:

An excellent refractory material made from used plaster-based mold investments which have been ground into a coarse grog. Its primary use is for making investment molds.

Notes

MACHINABILITY:

The degree of ease or difficulty of machining a material. For example, a magnesium alloy may be comparatively easy to machine while tool steel is difficult.

MACHINING:

In general, this term refers to the use of power driven machinery to cut away the surface of metal.

MAGNESIUM:

One of man's lightest, strongest metals. It is obtained from the oceans and is silver-white in color. It is easily worked by ordinary metalworking techniques and maintains a high ratio of strength to weight. Magnesium wheels are commonly used on high speed, competitive racing cars where light weight and strength are critical.

MALLEABILITY:

A metal's capability of being shaped, forged, extended or rolled in all directions without breaking or cracking. Gold is the most highly malleable metal. Metals in descending order of malleability are gold, silver, aluminum, copper, tin, platinum, lead, zinc (hot), wrought iron, and soft steel.

MANDREL:

A type of tapered, metal-forming stake used for sizing, stretching and shaping rings and bracelets. Silversmiths use cone-shaped and truncated cone-shaped mandrels for box work, hollow ware, trays, or any work requiring a firm, flat surface. These stakes are made of hardened steel and are finished to a fine, soft luster.

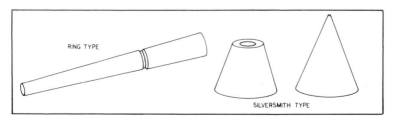

RING TYPE

SILVERSMITH TYPE

MANGANESE STEEL:
An alloy of steel first developed in 1882 by Sir Robert Hadfield. Containing about one percent carbon and thirteen percent manganese, this alloy is one of the hardest and most resilient known to man. It has been used for constructing military steel helmets, chains, rock and ore crushers, steam shovels and safes.

MAPP GAS (Methylacetylene Propadiene):
Originally developed by Dow Chemical Company in 1964, this welding fuel compound offers a versatility that rivals acetylene. For many jobs Mapp has proven itself already to be a worthwhile replacement for acetylene. Perhaps its outstanding feature is its safe handling qualities. A dropped cylinder of Mapp will not explode from the impact or shock. Comparatively, water and Mapp possess an equivalent resistance to shock. Used in combination with oxygen for welding, Mapp virtually eliminates backfire or flashback that is commonly encountered during oxy-acetylene welding. If comparable quantities of Mapp and acetylene were placed in cylinders side by side, the Mapp cylinder would be smaller and lighter.

MECHANICAL JOINING:
Any method of joining parts by fastening with bolts, screws, rivets, crimps, clamps, staples or bands.

MELTING RATE:
The speed at which an electrode is consumed during arc welding. Melting rate may be measured by reduction in weight or length of electrode consumed per unit time.

METAL-ARC CUTTING:
The heat of the electric arc may be used for cutting as well as for joining metals. To cut metal, the welding machine's current adjustment is set well above what is normally required for most joining processes. The increased current enables the welder to use the electrode as a knife or gouge to penetrate metal. The disadvantage of arc cutting is that the cuts tend to be very rough and the process generates a great deal of molten spatter.

METAL-ARC (WELDING):
A consumable metal electrode supplies the filler metal for this welding process. Coalescence or fusion of metal parts is brought about by heat from the arc generated between an electrode and the work.

90

METAL ELECTRODE: (See: ELECTRODE)

METALLOID:

A semi-metal element which behaves under certain conditions as a metal, and under other conditions as a non metal. Boron is an example of a metalloid or semi-metal.

METALLURGY:

An area of science and technology which deals with the economical extraction of metals from ores, and the application of these metals to various uses.

MICROMETER:

A highly accurate device used for measuring metal stock to the nearest one thousandth of an inch. There are three commonly used types of micrometers: outside, inside, and depth. The outside micrometer measures external dimensions such as the diameter of a piece of bar stock. The inside micrometer measures internal diameters of tubes, holes, cylinder bores, or the width of practically any recess. The depth micrometer measures the depth of holes or recesses.

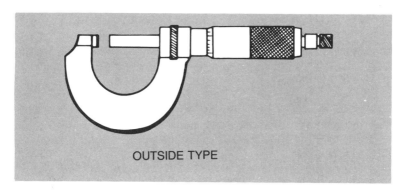

OUTSIDE TYPE

MIG WELDING: (See: GAS METAL-ARC WELDING)

MILD STEEL:

The carbon content of steel determines whether it is hard and brittle or highly ductile. Mild steel has a very low carbon content (up to .25 percent) and is highly ductile. Steel bridge girders and ship's plate are strong but pliant mild alloys of steel. Mild steel is easily worked and possesses a wide range of possible applications. For this reason mild steel alloys are the most widely used metals for welding.

MILLING MACHINE:

A machine which removes metal from work pieces by means of rotary cutters. (See: CUTTER [Milling]).

MISRUN:

This is a casting failure which occurs when cast metal is poured too cold so that it freezes before filling the mold entirely.

MIXING CHAMBER:

The valve is a gas welding or oxygen cutting torch where oxygen and acetylene gases are combined.

MOHS SCALE:

Friedrich Mohs, a 19th century mineralogist, originated a rather impressive hardness system that measured the ability of one mineral to be scratched by another. For example, Mohs deducted that since tungsten carbide will not scratch silicon carbide, but silicon carbide will scratch tungsten carbide, silicon carbide is the harder of the two.

MOKUME:

An old Japanese ironworking technique wherein layers of variously composed iron were forge-welded together into a laminated block or sheet especially for use in sword and sword guard making. This sandwich of metal was typically etched in an acid bath so that it resembled the varied grain of wood. This rough appearance was greatly admired, and was often used as a background or support for precious metal decorations.

MOLD WASH:

A water-soluble emulsion made from silica flour, graphite, carbon, and other substances. By coating the inside surface of a plaster mold with mold wash, good definition and easy separation from the mold is insured.

MOLYBDENUM STEEL:

When molybdenum is used as an alloying agent in steel, the steel produced resists very high pressures and temperatures. In recent years, molybdenum has been replacing tungsten in high-speed steels. It takes much less molybdenum than tungsten to produce a steel alloy of comparable strength. This alloy is used for automotive parts, for wire as fine as .01 mm (.0004 in) in diameter, and for ball and roller bearings.

MONEL METAL:

A nickel alloy composed of 67 percent nickel and 30 percent copper with small percentages of iron, manganese, carbon, silicon, and sulphur. Monel melts at 1305°-1350°C (2370-2460°F). It is highly resistant to corrosion from acids, alkalies, and food products in moist and dry atmospheres.

MONKEY WRENCH:

An ajustable wrench especially designed for turning octagonal and square-headed nuts and bolts. The jaws of this wrench are smooth and therefore unsuitable for turning pipe, rods or other round work. One jaw of this wrench remains stationary while the other is movable. One 12 inch to 18 inch variety of this wrench used by structural ironworkers is called a spud wrench.

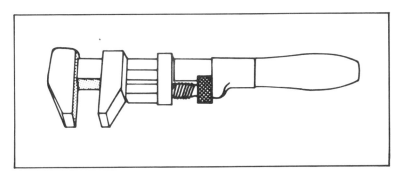

MUNTZ BRASS:

An alloy consisting of 60 percent copper and 40 percent zinc. Its melting point is 900°C (1650°-2460°F) and its principal use is for brazing rods and hot forging. It is also used in maritime and decorative architectural situations where corrosion resistance is a consideration.

MUSIC WIRE:

A carbon steel wire from which springs are manufactured.

Notes

NAVAL BRASS:
An alloy of 60 percent copper, 39.25 percent zinc, and 0.75 percent tin. Its melting point is 900°C (1630°F). It is used for welding rods and many other applications.

NEEDLE FILE:
A smaller and finer version of the standard metal files. Most are sword shaped though other shapes are used for special tasks.

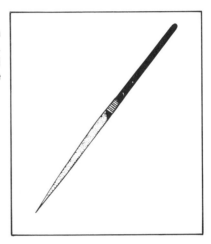

NEUTRAL FLAME: (See: FLAME, NEUTRAL)

NICHROME WIRE:
An alloy of nickel which is used for the heating element wire in electric kilns. It has a high electrical resistance.

NICKEL STEEL:
The addition of nickel to steel results in an alloy which is stronger than ordinary steel plate. The U.S. Navy uses a nickel steel alloy for armour plate on ships. It has been used for various components in automobiles and other vehicles where shock and wear resistance are important. Nickel steel is also an effective rust retardant.

NIELLOING:
A process wherein sulfur-containing compounds plus metal oxides are used to create contrasting effects between the darkened recesses and the raised bright surfaces of silver.

NITRIDING:

This is a casehardening technique during which an alloy of steel is heated while it is in a special airtight chamber where ammonia gas has been introduced at a high temperature. The alloy absorbs nitrogen in the form of nitrides which give extreme hardness to the surface.

NOBLE METALS:

The metals referred to here are those such as pure gold, silver, and platinum which retain comparatively unchanged surfaces despite atmospheric variations.

NONFERROUS ALLOYS:

Metal alloys which contain iron are ferrous, and those alloys containing any metal except iron are called nonferrous.

NORMALIZING:

Frequently during welding, forming or machining operations stresses develop in ferrous metals which must be relieved. This is accomplished by heating the metal to approximately 37.8°C (100°F) above its critical temperature range and then slow cooling it in still air at room temperature.

O

OIL HARDENING:
The cold hardness of a piece of hot steel depends on the method and rate of cooling. The hardening of steel in a mineral oil bath results in less distortion than quenching or cooling in water, because cooling is slower in oil.

ORE:
Any mineral from which metal can be extracted economically.

OVERHEAD POSITION (Welding):
This welding position is the most difficult for the welder to manage, because joints are welded from the underside. Beyond the awkwardness of the position, gravity tends to pull molten bits of slag and metal down on the welder. When welding in this position, special care must be taken by the welder to protect his arms, hands, face and eyes.

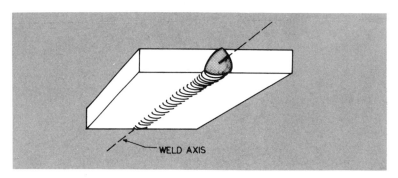

WELD AXIS

OXIDE (Finishes):
The tendency of metals to form surface oxides or salts may be used to create permanent and semipermanent colored finishes. By applying chemicals and sometimes heat, copper, bronze and iron may be colored. There are ready-mixed commercial oxidizing solutions available from chemical suppliers.

OXIDIZING FLAME: (See: FLAME, OXIDIZING)

OXY-ACETYLENE CUTTING:

A flame cutting process which depends upon the chemical reaction of oxygen with iron bearing metal. This reaction is known as oxidation; it is the same reaction that produces rust in nature. In oxy-acetylene flame cutting, oxidation is speeded up so dramatically that when the pre-heated iron bearing metal oxidizes it simply burns away, leaving ashes, or slag. This rapid cutting or oxidation is brought about by the high temperatures achieved when acetylene and oxygen gases are burned at the tip of a specially designed torch.

OXY-ACETYLENE WELDING:

A welding process which uses the flame from a burning oxygen and acetylene gas mix to join ferrous metal parts by melting pieces together into a homogeneous mass. A filler metal may or may not be used.

OXYGEN PRESSURE-ADJUSTING SCREW:

A thumbscrew having a large round or flat-sided head. It regulates oxygen pressure for welding or cutting. A clockwise turning increases oxygen pressure to whatever working pounds per square inch a job requires.

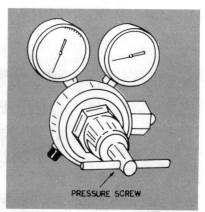

PRESSURE SCREW

PADDING:

A process in which beads are welded side by side and parallel. This process is used industrially to raise the surface of worn or broken parts.

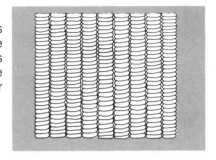

PARTING:

The separation of metal into two sections or pieces.

PARTING LINE:

A narrow line on a casting indicating the separation between the parts of a multiple piece mold. In sand casting this line shows where the cope and drag meet. It is removed from casting by chasing and filing processes.

PARTING SAND:

A finely ground or powdered foundry sand that is dusted on the sand in the drag in order to make separation from the cope easier. A burned molding sand is sometimes used for the purpose of parting.

PASS:

Each time the welder "runs a bead" he also makes a pass. A pass is a single welding operation during which a weld is made along a joint or along another weld deposit.

PATTERN:

In sand casting the pattern is the form around which the sand for creating a mold is packed. After it has been packed, the form is usually removed leaving a mold cavity into which molten metal is poured. Patterns are typically made of wood, although sculptors frequently use a styrofoam pattern which is left in the packed sand mold until it disintegrates in the heat of the pour.

PATTERN WEAVING:

A process wherein multiple sheets of different steels are alternately layered and forge welded together. The laminated appearance of pattern welded material makes it easily recognizable. Beautiful and dramatically varied patterns are possible depending on the forging technique used and the composition of the alternating layers of metal.

PEENING:

The stretching and shaping of metal by hammering, most often using the rounded end of a ball-peen or forming hammer.

PEWTER: (See: BRITANNIA METAL; GAR ALLOY)

PICKLING:

The acid cleaning of metal and removing of firescale which forms on metal during heat treating and soldering. A commonly used bath for gold and copper consists of ten parts water and one part sulphuric acid or eight parts water to one part nitric acid.

PIG:

An ingot of metal, usually iron, that is remelted in a furnace or crucible for casting. Originally, iron workers thought these ingots, as they were poured from the furnace, bore a resemblance to the animal, hence the name.

PINCH BAR: (See: CROWBAR)

PINCHBECK METAL:

An alloy of 88 percent copper and 12 percent zinc which was used as a gold substitute by Victorian jewelers because of its strong resemblance to gold. Red brass is the closest contemporary alloy to pinchbeck in use. It is 85 percent copper and 15 percent zinc and is used for making costume jewelry.

PINHOLE POROSITY:

A common fault in castings characterized by a sprinkling of small holes due to the escape of gas in the metal as it cools and shrinks.

PINNING:

This is a strong way of fastening metal pieces which has the advantage of being removable. Flat, wedge-shaped metal pins are hammered into pre-formed, tapered holes. Pins are of value for joining units that must be taken apart and reassembled.

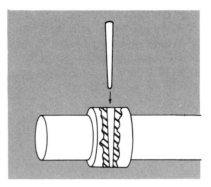

PIN SPANNER WRENCH:

This wrench is very much like a hook spanner except that it has a pin on the end of its curved arm instead of a hook. This pin fits into a round hole in the outer edge of the nut to allow loosening or tightening of the nut. (See: HOOK SPANNER)

PIPE CUTTER:

A hand-operated tool used for cleanly cutting metal pipe and tubing. It has a cutting wheel made from a hardened steel alloy such as nichrome. Some cutters come equipped with a tool steel reamer for smoothing the inside edge of freshly cut pipe.

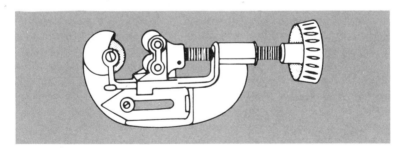

PIQUE WORK:

A decorative metalworking process used in Victorian England wherein fine gold or silver wire was hammered or inlaid in tortoise shell. Interest in this technique by contemporary craftsmen has revived its use. Today, gold and silver are inlaid in bone, horn, shell, ivory and plastic in addition to tortoise shell.

PIT:

A sharp surface depression in metal.

PITCH:

Refers to the distance between the points or crests
of adjacent screw threads.

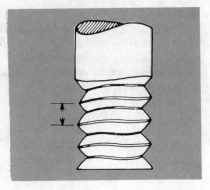

PLANISHING:

That part of the metal raising process which involves
smoothing and finishing a raised shape. A special planishing
hammer and an anvil or stake is used; the shape is
hammered systematically. (See: HAMMER)

PLASMA-ARC WELDING, CUTTING:

This welding-cutting process was discovered by Robert M.
Gage in 1953. Gage, a welding development engineer, found
that when a long electrical arc is forced through a small
torch nozzle by a hot ionized gas traveling at high speeds,
the resulting constricted arc could reach temperatures of up
to 27,600°C (50,000°F). Also, this arc could be finely tuned for
clean cutting of very thin metals. Prior to the invention of
plasma-arc cutting, aluminum could only be cleanly cut by
slow and expensive mechanical means.

PLASTICITY:

The capacity of a metal to be extensively deformed without
breaking.

PLATE:

The term "plate" refers generally to any sheet metal which
exceeds 3.18 mm (1/8 in) thickness.

PLATEN (Welding):
A cast iron or steel work surface used for welding, bending or holding metal. The platen consists of a grid of evenly spaced one and one half inch square holes, and has a machined top for accurate and precison work. Bending posts, pins and clamps may be placed in the grid with flexibility and efficiency.

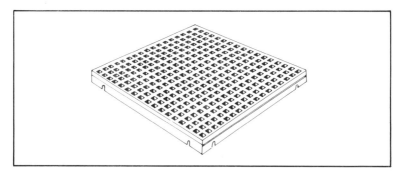

PLATING:
A group of processes wherein a base metal receives a thin metallic coating. This coating protects the base metal from corrosion and may also be used to obtain a beautiful finish over the base metal.

PLIERS, VISE-GRIP SELF-LOCKING:
A hand tool used for gripping or holding. It has a self-locking, adjustable jaw, and is often used instead of the less convenient screw type clamp.

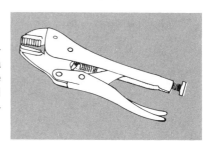

PLUG WELD:
A circular weld made through a hole in one or in some instances both pieces of metal to be joined. Typically, a plug weld is used to weld two metal plates which are to be joined in a lap or tee joint. (See: SLOT WELD)

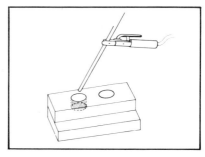

PLUMBAGO:

A compound of clay and powdered graphite from which crucibles for melting metals are made.

PLUMB BOB:

A rounded, tapered, sharp pointed brass or bronze weight which is suspended from a length of string in order to accurately determine the vertical line from a point at ground level. Plumb bobs are manufactured in weights of 170 - 680 g (6 - 24 oz.)

POPPING:

A common welding fault which results when the gas pressure used to operate the torch is less than what is required by the size of the torch tip. Popping also occurs when the tip is overheated, when the tip touches the work, or when the tip's opening is blocked by debris.

POP RIVETER:

A mechanically or hydraulically-operated hand tool for riveting light gage metals. Steel or aluminum pop type rivets are used. These rivets are usually available in diameters which vary from 3.18 to 4.76 mm ($1/8$ to $3/16$ in).

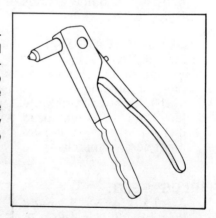

POROSITY:

A general term describing the faulty condition of castings which contain blowholes and cavities caused by shrinkage, trapped gas or gas in the molten metal. Improper melting, improper venting or overheating may cause this condition.

POURING GATE:

The widened funnel or cup-shaped investment opening into which molten metal is poured directly from the crucible. It serves as a reservoir for the metal and insures a steady even flow of metal through the sprue system.

POWDER METALLURGY: (See: SINTERING)

PREHEATING:

The application of heat to the base metal immediately before welding, brazing, soldering or cutting. Preheating metal will improve weld quality and help compensate for weld distortion. Also, preheating aids in the prevention of crack formation in the weld area.

PRITCHEL HOLE:

A 9.5—15.9 mm ($^3/_8$ - $^5/_8$ in) hole in the anvil face which in horseshoeing days was used to form studs for insertion into horseshoes. Modern smiths use the hole to accommodate special tools and operations. (See: ANVIL)

PROPANE TORCH:

Propane is a liquified petroleum gas which is most often used for jobs requiring a flame heat of under 540°C (1000°F). Certain kinds of soft and hard soldering may be readily accomplished using a portable propane cylinder and torch.

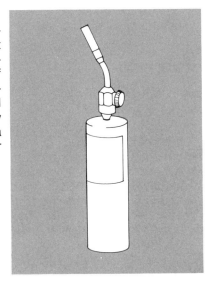

PUNCH AND MATRIX:

The positive and negative units used in the die stamping process. Each unit is designed to fit closely into the other, so that stamping will produce a clean, sharp outline.

PUNCH (Hand):

This tool is held in the hand and struck on one end with a hammer. Punches are designed to mark metal softer than the point end, drive and remove pins and rivets, and align holes in different metal sections. Most punches are made of tool steel. The hand held portion of the punch is either octagonal in shape or knurled in order to prevent its slipping. The center punch is the most commonly used metalworking punch. The center punch, as the name infers, is used for marking the center of a hole to be drilled. It is also used for marking metal during layout work.

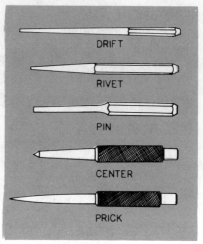

PUNCHING:

The use of a punch and die to cut holes in sheet metal.

PUNCHWORK:

A sheet metal decorating technique which uses punches of two general types. The first type of punch is smooth, polished and has a definite shape such as round, square, oval or diamond. It is worked usually from the back of the metal. The second type of punch imprints a design or pattern and is worked from the front of the metal. The design motif may be a single unit or an overall repeat pattern. These punches are traditionally used for textural effects and for background work.

PYROMETALLURGY:

A branch of metallurgy dealing with the chemical reduction of metals from ores. This reduction process involves melting the ores and chemically combining the unwanted elements. (See: SMELTING)

106

PYROMETER:

A device for measuring the high temperatures generated in kilns and crucibles. It uses a thermocouple which converts heat into electric current which in turn is measured in order to determine temperature.

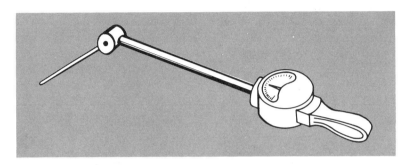

Notes

Q

QUENCH HARDENING:

This is a process which substantially increases a ferrous alloy's hardness by heating it within or above its transformation range then cooling it at a specific rate.

QUENCHING:

A method of rapid cooling heated metal by dipping in oil or water. This action decreases malleability making the metal more brittle.

QUENCHING OILS:

The vegetable, animal and mineral oils which are used in heat treating metals. Fish oil may be used, but it produces an offensive odor. These oils are usually compounded and sold under a variety of trade names.

Notes

RAISING:

A basic silversmithing method of shaping and forming hollow ware from flat sheets of metal by compression. This compression is effected by hammering the metal by slow stages on anvils or stakes into hollow forms of almost any contour.

RAMMER:

A wooden mallet or tool used to pack the sand around a pattern in foundry work.

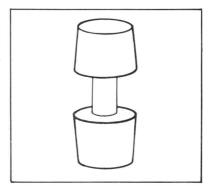

REAMER:

A cutting tool used to produce smooth, accurate, finely-finished holes by removing small amounts of metal from roughly cut or drilled holes.

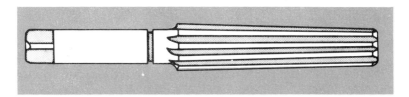

RECIPROCATING POWER HACKSAW:

This hacksaw derives its name from the repetitive back and forth action of its power driven blade. The saw's variable-speed motor allows its blade to cut at speeds from zero to several thousand strokes per minute. (See: BAYONET SAW)

RED BRASS: (See: PINCHBECK METAL)

REDUCING FLAME: (See: FLAME, CARBURIZING)

REGULATOR (Reducing Valve):
The set of gages and valves which control the flow of oxygen and acetylene used in flame welding. The regulator delivers gases to the torch under a constant pressure regardless of fluctuations in the cylinder pressure of the gas (See: ACETYLENE PRESSURE-ADJUSTING SCREW, OXYGEN PRESSURE-ADJUSTING SCREW)

REPOUSSE:
The chasing of a flat sheet of metal from the back using various hand punches.

RESISTANCE WELDING:
A group of welding processes which utilize the heat created from the resistance of a weld metal to an electric current moving through a circuit. The metal to be welded is a part of the electrical circuit and pressure is applied to assist joining. These processes are used on a broad basis for industrial production work. Resistance welding is rarely useful to the individual craftsman. (See: SPOT WELDING)

REVERSE POLARITY:
Adjusting the polarity on a direct current arc welding machine is a useful means for controlling weld penetration and heat. Reverse polarity welding concentrates arc heat on the work rather than on the electrode, therefore deep penetration of the base metal is possible and thick sections may be easily welded. For reverse polarity welding, the work piece or ground becomes electrically negative and the electrode positive.

RIFFLER:
A special variety of file used by the steel engraver and silversmith. Especially effective for reaching difficult corners and bends. The filing of inside surfaces and the enlargement of holes is expediently handled when this small, curved rasp or file is used.

RISER:

A vent which permits the escape of gases generated during casting. If these gases are not vented, they may be trapped during the pour. A riser is also a reservoir of molten metal provided to compensate for the contraction of molten cast metals as they solidify.

RIVET:

A short piece of cylindrical metal consisting of a head and a shank. It is produced in four general types: (1) button head, (2) conical head, (3) steeple head, and (4) countersunk. The diameter of the shank should be equal to twice the thickness of the metal being riveted.

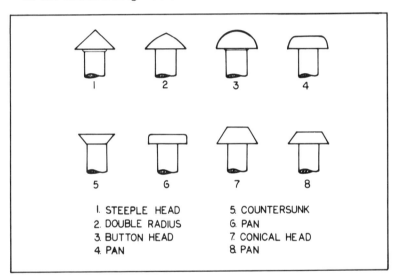

1. STEEPLE HEAD
2. DOUBLE RADIUS
3. BUTTON HEAD
4. PAN
5. COUNTERSUNK
6. PAN
7. CONICAL HEAD
8. PAN

RIVETING:

The process of clinching or bending rivets. Smaller rivets are clinched cold, while the larger varieties must be heated to soften the metal (See: POP RIVETER)

ROCKWELL HARDNESS TEST:

This is a method of analyzing a metal's hardness which involves the use of a machine to penetrate a test specimen with either a steel ball or a diamond spheroconical penetrator. The metal's hardness is determined by relating indentation depths to Rockwell Hardness numbers. The deeper the indentation, the softer the metal and the lower the Rockwell number.

RODS (Welding):

Good welded joints often require the addition of a filler metal. This metal is manufactured in the form of wire rods of varying diameters. Welding rods may be flux coated or bare. The welder chooses a rod according to its diameter and physical properties. The alloy of the rod selected must be compatible with the metal to be joined if good fusion is expected.

ROOT CRACK:

A fracture in the area of the root of a welded joint.

ROOT OF JOINT:

The root of a joint which has been prepared for welding is the deepest part of a joint, or that part of a joint where the pieces come closest to each other. Viewed in cross section the root may be a point, a line, or an area.

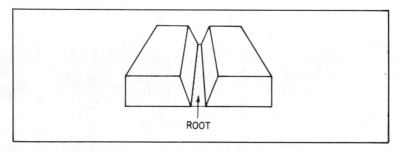

ROOT

ROOT OF WELD:

The area or points where the back of the weld spans both base metal surfaces.

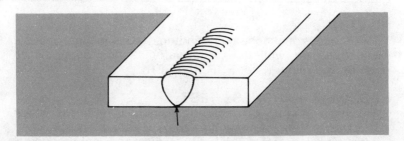

ROOT OPENING:

The space separating the pieces to be joined at the root of the joint.

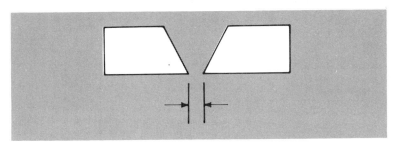

RUNNERS:

The main feeder channels which conduct molten metal from the pouring gate into the mold cavity.

RUNOUT:

The loss or escape of molten metal from a mold, furnace or melting crucible.

Notes

SAE:
An abbreviation which stands for the Society of Automotive Engineers. This organization maintains a broad ranging list of steel alloys using code numbers that indicate the composition of each type.

SAFE EDGE:
Refers to that edge of a file which has no teeth.

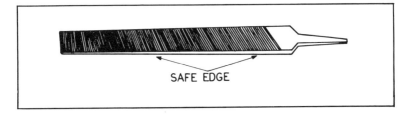

SAFE EDGE

SAL AMMONIAC (Ammonium Chloride):
A corrosive soft soldering flux especially useful for soldering iron, steel, stainless steel, zinc, and galvanized iron.

SANDBLASTING;
A cleaning process wherein sand is blown under very high air pressure at a metal surface.

SAND BURNING:
The hard surface or crust resulting from contact between molten metal and the sand mold surface during casting.

SAND MOLD CASTING:
A process which involves pouring molten metal into a cavity that has been formed in a mold made from specially tempered and dampened sand.

SCAB (Scabby):
A casting flaw which is caused by the eruption of gas from the face of the mold. It may also be brought about by uneven mold surfaces or it may occur as a result of splashing molten metal on mold walls during a pour.

SCALE:

An undesirable oxide coating that forms on heated metals. It may be removed by abrasive grinding or in the case of coatings by submersion in a pickling solution of sulphuric acid and water (sixty parts water to one part acid).

SCARFING:

A method of preparing iron or steel parts for forge welding. If, for instance, two lengths of iron are to be joined, the end of each length must be heated and hammered to thicken or flatten it. These thickened ends are called "scarfs" and when they are overlapped, properly heated and fluxed, they may be hammered together to form a strong welded joint.

SCORPER: (See: BURIN)

SCRAP:

Metal discard, or cuttings, or junk which can be reprocessed.

SCRATCH AWL:

A sharp, point-hardened steel tool used to mark or incise lines on metal. It is designed in many varied forms; one of the most prevalent is illustrated.

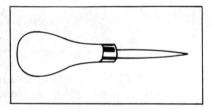

SCREW EXTRACTOR: (See: EZY-OUT)

SCREW PITCH GAGE:

This gage offers an accurate and easy method for determining the number of threads to the inch in a bolt, screw or a nut. The gage consists of a set of metal leaves. Each leaf is cut to match a specified thread size. When the gage user finds the right coincidence of a leaf with an unknown screw thread, the thread size is read from the identification printed on the leaf.

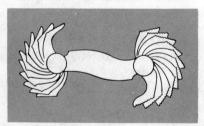

SCREWS (Machine):

Hundreds of screws, bolts and nuts of every design and description are commercially available. The craftsman's choice of a screw for joining metal parts will be made on the basis of functional and formal necessities. Generally, if light gage sheet metals are to be screwed into or assembled, a machine screw will do the job.

It would be an unlikely choice from a practical standpoint to join two pieces of light gage sheet metal using an eight inch track bolt. However, when the craftsman's formal or aesthetic necessities must be satisfied, a typical use of screws, bolts, and nuts may not be the best application.

Craftsmen have often used exposed screws, bolts, and nuts for decorative purposes in their work. Although a particular screw will meet the structural requirements of a work, the craftsman's design may necessitate using another screw because of its decorative appropriateness.

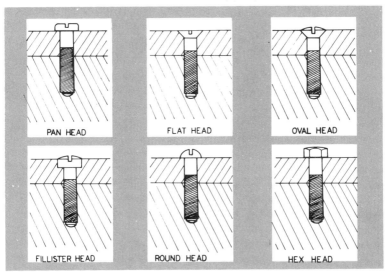

PAN HEAD   FLAT HEAD   OVAL HEAD

FILLISTER HEAD   ROUND HEAD   HEX HEAD

SCRIBE:

To draw or incise a line on metal with a scriber, scratch awl or other sharp-pointed tool.

SCRIBER: (See: SCRATCH AWL)

SECOND CUT FILE:

This file has mediumly spaced teeth. It cuts more smoothly than a bastard file and cuts more coarsely than a smooth file. It may be either single or double cut. (See: FILE)

SEMIBLIND JOINT:
A joint which has one hidden or nonvisible part.

SETSCREW: (See: ALLEN SCREW)

SET UP:
To position a workpiece, attachments and cutting tools on a machine tool in readiness for work.

SHAKE-OUT:
A term for the separation of castings from a mold. "Break-out" or "break-up" are comparable terms used in art foundry casting.

SHANK, CRUCIBLE: (See: CRUCIBLE SHANK)

SHEAR:
A machine for cutting metal products. There are many kinds of shears but they all operate on the same general principle as that used for shearing cloth or paper. The work rests upon a lower blade and an upper blade is brought down, severing the piece. A shear utilizes either an electric, manual or hydraulic drive. The shearing mechanism itself may be rotary, rocking, gate, guillotine or alligator type. (See: BENCH SHEAR)
The term shear may also be used to refer to a metal's capacity to resist the perpendicular action of the cutting blade of a shearing machine.

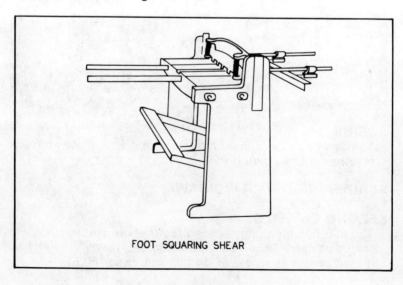

FOOT SQUARING SHEAR

SHEARS, METAL HAND:
These scissorslike tools are manufactured in a variety of designs and are used for cutting light gage sheet metal of all varieties. (See: AVIATION SNIPS)

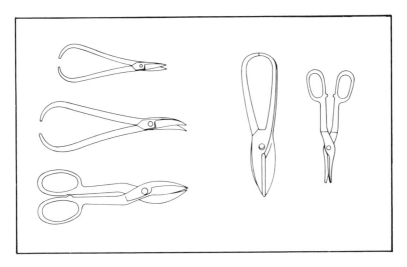

SHIM:
These are pieces of sheet metal or steel of various sizes which are slipped between mating parts to establish a desired clearance. These sheet metal pieces are available in a variety of thicknesses.

SHORTNESS:
The brittleness of a metal.

SHOTTING:
A method of preparing metal for casting or decorative uses. Molten metal is poured in drops from a crucible or ladle held at a height above a container of water. As the molten drops fall, they form pellets or "shot" which freeze into shape just before striking the surface of the water.

SIDE-CUTTING PLIERS (Sidecutters):

Used for holding, bending and cutting light gage metals or small gage wire. Electricians use this tool extensively for stripping insulation from wire and for splicing wire ends. The pliers' cutting jaws are located just forward of the pivotal joint and are hollowed out on one side.

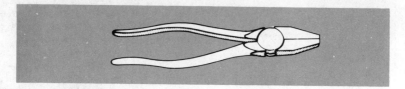

SILVER SOLDER:

A hard solder used most frequently in jewelry making and repair. It is an alloy consisting usually of copper, zinc and silver. The alloy must contain at least 8 percent silver. Its working temperature ranges between 600-870°C (1112°-1598°F).

SINGLE CUT FILE:

This variety of file has rows of teeth which are cut parallel to each other at an angle of approximately 65 degrees. Fine finishing, blade sharpening and drawfiling are tasks suited to this type of file. The rough edges of sheet metal may be best smoothed using a single cut file. (See: FILE)

SINKING:

A method for creating a volumetric form by hammering a flat metal sheet into a mold. The metal is stretched or forced into the mold by hammering it from the concave side.

SINTERING:

An industrial technique for fabricating parts from metal powders. The powder is heated and compacted in a press which may apply pressure ranging from fifteen to fifty tons.

SKIMMER:

A tool used to skim off dirt or surface impurities from the top of molten metal. Also, during a crucible pour it prevents slag from running with the molten metal into the mold.

SKULL:

A thin film of casting metal which remains in the crucible or ladle after excess has been poured into pig molds for future use.

SLAG:

Metal dross which results from the action of a flux upon undesirable oxidized constituents of metal.

SLAG INCLUSION:

Solid, nonmetallic impurities trapped either between the weld metal and the base metal or in the weld metal.

SLIDING T-BEVEL:

This tool is basically an adjustable try square used for laying out angles which are other than 90 degrees. It may also be used for checking constructed angles.

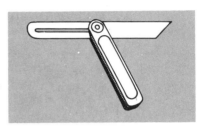

SLIP-JOINT PLIERS:

The most commonly available pliers are the slip-joint or adjustable type. These pliers are designed so that by manually dislocating the jaws the user can increase the opening and gripping range.

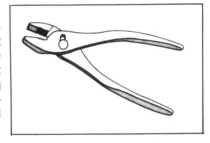

SLOT WELD:

A weld which utilizes a bored or cut slot in one of the pieces of metal to be joined. The weld metal is deposited in the slot on one piece of a lap or tee joint, fusing that piece to the exposed section of the other underlying piece (See: PLUG WELD)

SLUSH CASTING:

A hollow casting technique used with metals having a low melting point and a wide freezing range; white metal (92% tin, 8% antimony) is one such metal. The metal is poured while it is molten into a cold mold and allowed to make contact with all surfaces. The metal that touches the mold freezes, forming a shell. Immediately, the mold is inverted and the remainder of the metal is poured out, leaving a hollow cast form.

SMELTING:

The operation by which metals are separated from the waste elements in ores by the application of heat and chemical energy. (See: PYROMETALLURGY)

SNARLING IRON:

A form of metal raising stake having a long arm (approximately 16″) terminating in a small, rounded or peen end. The arm is inserted into narrow or long-necked hollow ware to assist in raising or forming.

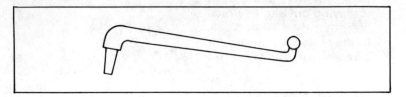

SOFT SOLDER:

Usually an alloy of tin and lead which melts at between 183° and 318°C (360° and 600°F). The melting temperature depends upon the ratio of tin to lead in the alloy.

SOFT SOLDERING (Methods):

Four methods of soft soldering metal joints may be identified: (1) General area or simultaneous heat approach—parts to be joined are placed together, flux and solder applied, everything is heated until the solder runs, (2) Soldering Iron—utilizes a heated copper tip which is dipped in flux. Preheating of the parts to be joined is necessary, (3) Sweating—method for joining broad surfaces. Surfaces are fluxed, then "tinned", that is, coated with a film of soft solder. Then surfaces are placed in contact and reheated so that solder will flow through the whole joint, (4) Wiping—Used by plumbers. Solder contains two parts lead and one part tin and is completely fluid at about 250° C (480° F), and completely solid at about 194°C (380°F). When it is "pasty" between 194° and 250°C (380° and 480°F) it is molded by hand pressure into shape.

SOLDERING (General):

All of the processes used for joining metal to metal by the use of a nonferrous low-melting point metal or alloy. The solder is applied in a molten state to the cleaned and prepared joint. Drawn by capillary attraction the solder flows between the parts of the joint and forms a surface alloy with the metal being soldered.

124

SOLDERING BLOCK:

Any work surface for soldering which retains heat well, allows work to be pinned easily, and does not break down quickly under repeated applications of heat and flame. Charcoal, asbestos and a composite material made of carbonate of magnesium and asbestos fiber are all excellent surfaces for soldering.

SOLDERING GUN:

An electric soldering tool having a pistol grip and a trigger which functions as a heat control. This tool is mainly useful for light duty soldering applications such as those in television electronics.

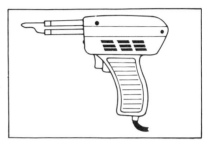

SOLDERING IRON:

This is a tool which is used for preheating metals which are to be joined and for melting the solder alloy. The soldering iron has a copper bit which may be either internally or externally heated. Internal heating is usually electrical. External heating is usually from a gas flame.

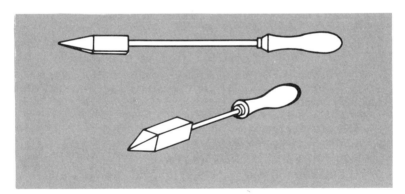

SOLIDUS:

The temperature at which a metal begins to melt as it is being heated. May also refer to the temperature at which a metal freezes during cooling.

SPALLING (Drop):

A serious casting defect which results from the collapse of an interior part of a plaster mold during the pouring of the metal.

SPANNERS:

Some unique nuts are made which have notches or holes cut into their outer edge or face. In order to loosen or tighten such nuts, specially designed wrenches called "spanners" must be used. (See: HOOK SPANNER, PIN SPANNER, FACE PIN SPANNER)

SPARK TEST:

An iron or steel sample may be held to a grinding wheel and the color and configuration of the sparks produced will assist in identifying the sample. For instance, wrought iron when it is held to the grinding wheel will give off long straw colored lines which are virtually free of spark bursts. A high carbon steel will give off yellow lines and very clear bright spark bursts.

SPATTER:

The metal chips and particles which are thrown off during welding and do not form part of the weld.

SPELTER:

These are brazing solders made from copper-zinc alloys which have comparatively low melting points, 710°C to 1120°C (1304°F to 2050°F). Used in conjunction with a welding torch, spelters of various colors and melting points may be used to join steel, copper, brass, and bronze while closely matching them in tint.

SPINNING (Metal):

A method of forming hollow bodies from disk shaped metal sheets. The technique involves the use of a lathe. The sheet metal is worked over a continuously turning wooden or metal shape which is basically round or at times oval. A tool is pressed against the revolving disc and it is gradually forced down over the wood or metal chuck until it takes the shape of the chuck. Cups, vessels, dishes and bowls are commercially produced by this method.

SPLITTING:

The dividing of metal at the edges without the loss of any metal. A hammer and chisel are used to open or split the metal cold or in a red hot state. Blacksmiths have long used this technique in decorative, forged and wrought iron work.

SPOT WELDING:

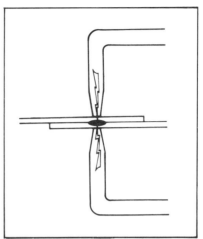

An electric-resistance welding process during which fusion is brought about at the interface where two metal pieces meet. The pieces being joined are pressed together between a pair of electrodes. An electrical charge of brief duration is passed through the metal joint between the electrodes and fusion occurs over a small arc. (See: RESISTANCE WELDING)

SPRAYING:

This is a metal plating process which involves the use of a special spray gun. A coating metal in wire or powder form is fed through the gun and is melted as it emerges. The hot liquid metal is blown by compressed air in minute droplets onto the surface to be coated. A preliminary roughening and cleaning of the metal to be plated is necessary to insure adhesion of the coating metal.

SPRUE:

An artery or channel which conducts molten metal from the pouring gate into the mold cavity. A sprue may also be employed to allow melted wax to run out of the mold investment during burn-out; and it may also be used to permit the escape of gas generated within the mold during pouring.

SPRUE SYSTEM:

A network of channels which connect the pouring gate with the mold cavity.

SPUD WRENCH:

A twelve to eighteen inch monkey wrench used by ironworkers to bolt structural steel framing together. (See: MONKEY WRENCH)

STAINLESS STEEL:

The addition of about ten to twenty percent chromium to steel results in this group of alloys which resist severe corrosion conditions and intense heat. Stainless steel is highly durable and is used for components in aerospace engineering. One alloy of stainless steel is used in the production of sinks and kitchen ware. In the United States stainless steel has found a wide range of architectural and artistic applications.

A favorite steel alloy of environmental sculptors, stainless is highly corrosion resistant and not readily altered by atmospheric conditions. A 12 to 30 percent chromium content in the alloy gives it its touch resistant qualities. Harry Brearley of Shelfield, England first discovered the corrosion and heat resisting character of chromium steel in 1913.

STAKE, METAL FORMING:

A shaping tool which is inserted into a steady block of hardwood, a special holder, or an anvil. Sheet metal is hammered over the stake and subsequently shaped in accordance with the degree of convexity of the face. Manufacturers produce almost endless variations of three basic stake designs (Anvil, T, and Mushroom). Several examples of each type are shown.

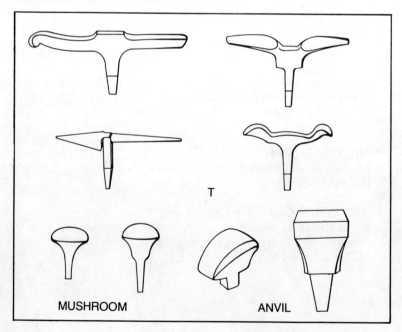

MUSHROOM   ANVIL

128

STEEL (Carbon Alloys):

The various carbon steel alloys are composed of quantities of carbon and smaller quantities of silicon, manganese, phosphorus, and sulfur. The amounts of carbon added to iron creates steels which vary greatly in strength and hardness. Because of carbon's importance as an alloying element, steel is separated into three sub-groupings which are designated low, medium and high carbon steels.

Low carbon steel contains about .05 to .30 percent carbon and is used for structural steel, automobile bodies, pipes, screws and nails. Also known as "mild" steel, low carbon steel is adaptable, highly ductile and has fine welding properties.

Medium carbon steel has .30 to .60 percent carbon and is therefore a stronger though less ductile alloy than those steels containing less carbon. It may be hardened by heat treatment and used in the manufacture of hammers, cold chisels, dies, and railroad rails. Medium carbon steel has less flexibility and toughness than low carbon steel and is more difficult to bend, weld and machine.

High carbon steel has a carbon content of above .60 percent. It is most frequently used as tool steel, and drills, taps, reamers, files and knives are made from it. In order to cut high carbon steel it must be annealed to make it soft and workable.

STELLITE:

This is an alloy of cobalt, chromium and tungsten used to make high speed cutting tools.

STERLING SILVER:

Silver alloyed with 7.5 percent copper is known as sterling. It has a lustrous silver-white color when polished. Its working qualities are splendid; it can be readily shaped and formed, and it hard solders well.

STRAIGHT POLARITY:

A direct current (D.C.) arc welding machine may be adjusted for straight polarity welding, sometimes called electrode negative, when light, thin metals are to be joined. The welding heat is focused in the electrode rather than in the base metal, therefore burn-through (too deep a penetration of metal) is less of a problem than is the case with D.C. reverse polarity welding. (See: REVERSE POLARITY)

STRESS:
The intensity, at any given point in a metal form, of the internal forces.

STRESS RELIEF HEAT TREATMENT:
Frequently, after making what appears to be a good weld, residual or locked-up stresses cause cracking and other defects in the metal. These defects may be avoided by postheating the weld metal to relieve the stress. Postheating of carbon or low alloy steel is done with a slightly carburizing flame at a temperature always below the critical range, about 427° to 508°C (1100°F to 1250°F), depending on the metal's thickness.

STRIKER: (See: FRICTION LIGHTER)

STRIKING THE ARC:
A continuous and stable electrical arc must be established between the electrode and the base metal in order to weld. Striking the arc involves scratching or tapping the tip of the electrode against the grounded base metal. To maintain the arc once it is struck and to avoid sticking, the electrode must be withdrawn from the base metal a distance approximately equal to the diameter of the electrode.

STRUCTURAL:
This term generically refers to all forms of iron and steel used in architectural construction.

SUBMERGED ARC WELDING:
This process is distinguished by the employment of a blanket of fine, granular fusible material on the work which acts as a shield for the arc. A base metal electrode is used and fusion is brought about by an arc between the electrode and the work. The electrode supplies the filler metal required for joining, although at times additional filler metal may be added from an extra rod.

SURFACE GAGE:

This tool is principally used for transferring measurements and scribing lines on metal. In the machine shop this gage may be handily used for laying out work. The gage is simply constructed; it is not calibrated, and consists of an adjustable scriber mounted on a heavy base.

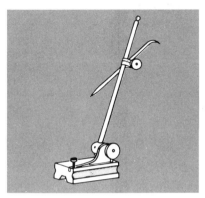

SWAGE:

Has two meanings: (A) To alter metal by hammering, rolling, bending or by any means other than cutting, (B) A two piece over and under tool used for finishing hot metal rods in convex shapes.

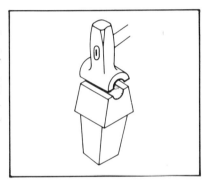

SWAGE BLOCK:

This is a basic forming tool used by metalworkers. It is simply a cast iron or steel block having grooves, depressions, shaped holes and surface patterns. Hot or cold metal stock may be shaped or punched when it is laid over an impression in the block. The block may weigh as much as 600 pounds.

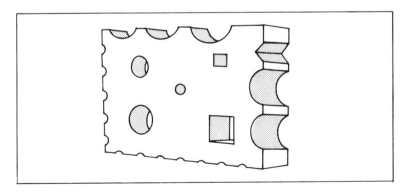

SWEATING:

A soldering technique. The surface of two pieces of metal which are to be joined are coated with solder, clamped together, then heated enough to melt the solder.

TACK WELD:
A holding weld which is usually temporary. This weld is most frequently used to hold parts in alignment until a more permanent weld can be made.

TANG:
The end of a file or graver upon which a handle may be placed. Also, the end of a metal raising stake which is inserted into a stump, anvil or other holding device.

TAP:
A tool used for cutting internal screw threads. Tapping may be done either by hand or by machine.

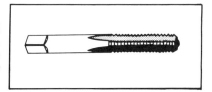

TAP WRENCH:
A manual tap holding and turning tool.

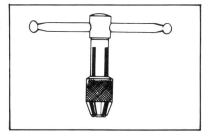

TAPE (Measuring):
An automatic or manually retractable measuring scale made usually of flexible metal, linen or cotton. These tapes are generally six feet or longer.

TARKASHI:
A style of brass wire inlay in wood practiced in India. Hardwood is used and ordinarily objects such as boxes, screens, trays, tables, and cabinet furniture are decorated in the technique. In India, tarkashi designs are usually derived from plant forms or geometric patterns.

TEE JOINT:

A tee joint is formed when two pieces of metal are set at right angles to each other in the shape of a T (See: JOINTS, BASIC WELDING)

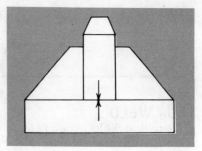

TELESCOPING GAGE:

Telescoping gages are T-shaped tools which are used for measuring the inside diameter of slots or holes. These gages are usually furnished in sets, the smallest gage measuring distances from 7.9 to 12.7 mm (5/16 to 1/2 in.), the largest gage measuring diameters from 90 to 150 mm (3½ to 6 in). The long arm of the T is used as a handle and the shorter crossarms are used for measuring. The spring-loaded crossarms are constructed so that they slide or telescope into each other. The arms are compressed, inserted into a hole to be measured, and allowed to expand. The tool is withdrawn, locked in position and the distance across the arms is measured.

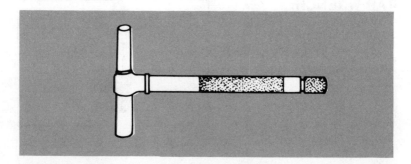

TEMPER:

When maximal toughness and flexibility are needed in steel, a tempering treatment is necessary. Basically, tempering involves warming hardened steel to a predetermined temperature for a given period of time. When the proper temperature has been reached the steel is quenched in oil or water to hold the temper.

TEMPLATE:

A pattern or guide.

134

TENSILE STRENGTH:

The ability of a metal to resist longitudinal stress and permanent deformation. The tensile strength of steel is usually expressed in neutons (pounds or tons per square inch).

THERMIT CRUCIBLE:

A magnesia tar lined metal vessel which is used for safely containing the thermit reaction and for transporting and pouring molten steel. The thermit crucible is usually made in the shape of an inverted cone with a tapping pin at the bottom.

THERMIT MIXTURE:

A powdered mixture of finely divided metal oxide and finely divided aluminum. Alloying elements may be added to the mixture as required.

THERMIT MOLD:

A typical mold consists of a mixture of high silica sand and plastic clay. These materials along with patterns for gates and risers are fitted into a box.

THERMIT REACTION:

Super heated molten steel may be produced by means of chemical reaction between a metal oxide and aluminum. This reaction is set off by introducing a highly flammable barium peroxide powder (thermit starter) into the metal oxide and aluminum mixture. The reaction will convert the powdered mixture into one ounce or one ton of liquid steel in less than half a minute.

THERMIT WELDING:

A welding process during which both the filler metal and the heat needed to bring about fusion comes from the molten steel produced by the chemical reaction between a metal oxide and aluminum.

THERMOPLASTIC ADHESIVE BONDING:

An adhesive material which is hardened by cooling and softened by heating. Metals bonded by these materials have excellent strength up to 65°C (150°F). Thermoplastic materials are most frequently used for bonding metal to non-metallic materials such as wood, leather, cork, paper, etc.

THERMOSETTING ADHESIVE BONDING:
An adhesive that hardens by the action of a non-reversible chemical reaction. Epoxy and alkyds are the most commonly used thermosetting materials for bonding metals.

THICKNESS (Feeler) GAGE:
The exact width of small openings may be measured using this device. It consists usually of from 2 to 26 blades. Each blade is a certain number of thousandths of an inch thick. Use of the gage requires simply inserting one or more of the blades between the points which define the width to be measured.

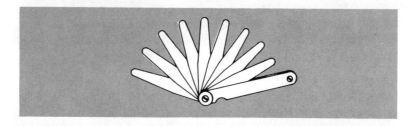

TIG WELDING: (See: GAS TUNGSTEN-ARC WELDING)

TIN:
A soft, shiny, silver-colored metal rarely used except as an alloy agent. Its main use is as an alloying metal with copper in the production of bronze. Tin is also the chief ingredient of pewter (britannia). It provides excellent protection against corrosion and is non-toxic.

TINNING:
Coating one metal with another either for the purpose of protection or decoration. In tinplate manufacturing this is the process of coating thin sheet metal with an even thinner layer of tin.

TINPLATE:
A thin sheet of steel coated with tin. The layer of tin is deposited either by electroplating or hot-dipping.

TIN SNIPS: (See: SHEARS, METAL HAND)

TIP CLEANER:

A tool used for cleaning the orifice opening of gas welding and cutting torches. Tip cleaners come as a package in assorted diameters. Each cleaner is serrated with an end file.

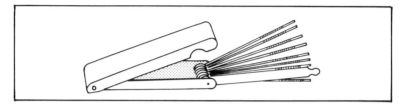

TITANIUM:

An alloy which bridges the gap between aluminum and steel. It is almost as strong as steel yet weighs only one half as much. This alloy, in addition to being lightweight, has high strength, and good temperature and corrosion resistance.

TOE CRACK:

A break in the base metal located at the toe of a weld.

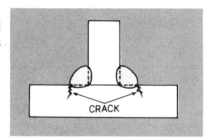

TOE OF WELD:

The point at which the face of the weld meets the base metal.

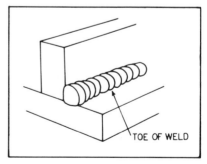

TONGS:

A tool designed for handling hot metal during shaping and heat treating operations. Forging tong jaws are shaped to accept different cross sections of rod and bar stock.

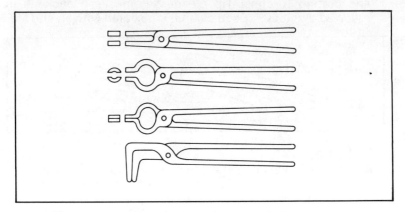

TONGS, CRUCIBLE: (See: CRUCIBLE TONGS)

TORQUE:

This is the amount of turning or twisting force that is applied to a threaded fastener.

TORQUE WRENCH:

A wrench that is used when a nut or bold must be tightened within specific limits. Accurate use of this wrench will prevent warp or undue stress on metal parts.

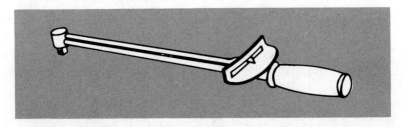

TOUCHSTONE:

One means of testing the purity of gold and silver is by rubbing a sample against this black, siliceous stone which is similar to flint or basanite. Once the touchstone has been rubbed hard enough to leave a visible deposit a process of chemical analysis is undertaken to determine the quality of the sample.

TRIP-HAMMER:
A metal forming machine which utilizes a cam drive assembly for alternately lifting and dropping a steel hammer head. Modern trip-hammers are usually electric powered and vary in size from twenty-five pounds for small units to huge industrial units weighing several tons. In small, modern forging operations this machine, eliminates the need for the striker or apprentice.

TRIPOLI:
A buffing compound, manufactured in stick form. It contains both a lubricant and abrasive and will help produce a lustrous finish on metal surfaces. (See: BUFFING)

TRY SQUARE:
This square is precisely made and is used to check lines or surfaces for squareness and for laying out work. It is made of two parts at right angles to each other. One part is a handle usually made of hardwood, and the other part is a thin, polished steel blade approximately eight inches in length. The blade is graduated in inches and fractions of an inch.

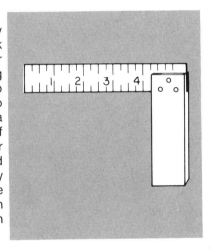

TUNGSTEN:
The most highly heat resistant metal known to man. It melts at 3420°C (6200°F). The high melting point of tungsten makes it very expensive to use with casting and melting processes. Shaping is almost exclusively done by powder metallurgy. It is used in making cutting tools. Also, for some years tungsten has been used to make automobile spark plug electrodes and engine breaker points.

TUNGSTEN CARBIDE:
The hardest man-made metal. Its hardness is only slightly less than that of a diamond. It is formed in a mold from a combination of tungsten and carbon under heat and pressure. Tools made by this process cut other metals faster than tools made from high speed steel.

TUNGSTEN ELECTRODE:

A permanent, non-consumable arc welding electrode which is made primarily of tungsten metal.

TUYERE:

The intake pipe or nozzle through which air is brought to the burning coals of a blacksmith's forge.

UNDERBEAD CRACK:
A subsurface break located beneath the weld bead within the heat affected zone.

UNDERCUTS:
This is any part of casting metal which would prevent separation of the mold parts without destroying either the obstructing portion of the model or the mold or both. This condition should be avoided when using two-piece molds, but may be solved when necessary by the use of a multiple-part mold. Another solution often preferred by craftsmen when unique castings are desired is reversion to one-piece molds.

UNDERFILL:
A surface depression in the face or root surface of a weld resulting from inadequate filling and poor welding technique.

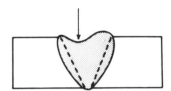

UNIVERSAL CHUCK: (See: CHUCK)

UPSETTING:
In forging this is a method for thickening and shortening a section of iron or steel by hammering one end while it is white hot.

UPSET WELDING:
An industrial welding process which fuses metal by utilizing pressure and heat created by the metal's resistance to electric current. Fusion occurs over the entire contact area of two butted surfaces. The process involves applying pressure before current is turned on and maintaining the pressure while the current heats the surface.

Notes

VANADIUM STEEL:

The addition of small amounts of vanadium to steel improves the steel's shock resistance and tensile strength. Chromium-vanadium steel has great tensile strength and is used for automotive springs, connecting rods, frames, axles, and other parts which require strength and flexibility.

V-BLOCK:

A square or rectangular steel block which has a 90 degree V accurately machined through its center. It may be used with a clamp for holding round stock for drilling, milling and laying out operations.

V-BOARD WITH CLAMP:

Sometimes referred to as a "wood bench pin," this device is used in conjunction with the jeweler's saw to support the metal being cut, filed, etc.

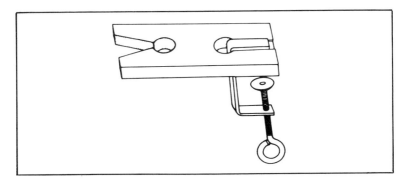

VENTS:

Narrow openings in closed mold investments which permit the escape of gases formed during a pour.

VERNIER CALIPER:

A precision measuring tool consisting of an L-shaped bar with a scale engraved on the long shank. A sliding jaw moves freely along the long shank and carries a jaw which matches the short arm of the L. The vernier scale permits measurements as accurate as .025 mm (.001 in). This tool is so delicate and requires such great care that its use is mainly confined to special applications where minute tolerances must be maintained.

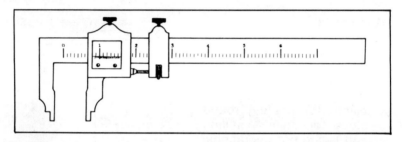

VERTICAL POSITION:

In vertical welding position the joint which is to be welded is upright, that is, the weld axis is approximately vertical.

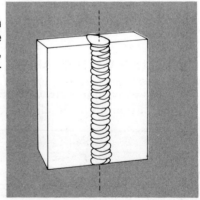

VIRGIN METAL:
Metal which has been directly taken from ore and never used before.

VISE CLAMPS (Soft-jaws):
These are hand-formed pieces of thin sheet copper or brass which are made to fit over and soften the hardened steel jaws of a vise in order to protect work from unnecessary scarring.

VISE, MACHINIST'S:
A mechanical work holding device which usually has one stationary and one adjustable jaw. It is available in weights ranging from thirty to two hundred pounds. (See: BLACK-SMITH'S VISE)

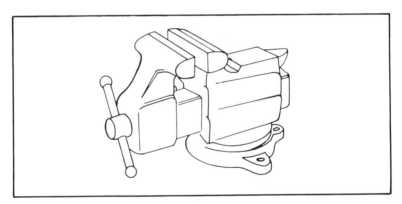

VOLTAGE REGULATOR:
An automatic electrical control in the arc welding machine which maintains an even flow of current to the primary windings of the transformer.

Notes

WARREN TRUSS:

A type of specially fabricated, "open" I-beam construction that is made of flat pieces of steel with round rod stock welded in the place of the typically solid I-beam web.

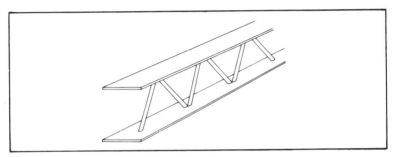

WEAVE BEAD:

A type of arc welded bead made by depositing the filler metal while using a side-to-side motion of the electrode. Several variations of the weave bead are possible.

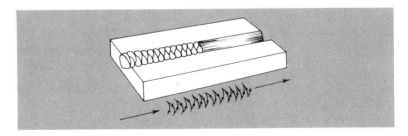

WELDABILITY:

Determination of the relative ease and effectiveness with which a metal may be welded into a particular form or structure.

WELD BEAD:
The weld metal deposit remaining after a weld pass.

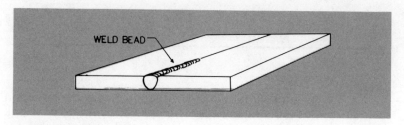

WELDED JOINT:
Any union of metal pieces produced by the application of a welding process. (See: JOINTS, BASIC WELDED)

WELDER: (See: WELDOR)

WELDING:
Any means of joining two pieces of metal by heating them to their melting point and allowing the molten metals to flow together and fuse as cooling occurs. Some processes involve the application of pressure and the use of a filler metal.

WELDING CYCLE:
The complete sequence of events which goes into the making of a given weld.

WELDING ROD:
A manufactured filler metal, in wire or rod form, used primarily in oxy-acetylene welding and brazing processes. Filler wire or rod is also used in those arc-welding processes wherein the electrode does not provide the filler metal.

WELDING, TRANSFORMER MACHINE:
This is the lightest, most compact and least expensive of the various electric arc welding machines. It lacks a polarity switch and produces only (A.C.) alternating current. This machine transforms current taken directly from an A.C. power line to the specific current required for welding.

WELDOR:

Author and former American Welding Society President, T. B. Jefferson has suggested this spelling of the word be adopted to refer to a person who is able to do manual or semiautomatic welding. The term "welder," Jefferson suggests, should be used only when the reference is to a welding machine.

WELD PENETRATION:

The depth of the weld.

WHEEL DRESSER:

A device used to true the face of a grinding wheel.

WHITE METAL:

An alloy consisting of 92 percent tin and 8 percent antimony. It melts at 246°C (475°F) and anneals at 200° and 241°C (392° and 437°F). Sheet and extruded wire are both made in this metal. One of its primary artistic and commercial uses is in the production of inexpensive costume jewelry. Also, a general term covering alloys that are based on tin, lead or antimony.

WIRE BRUSH:

A wooden-handled brush having bristles made of steel wire. It is used by weldors for cleaning rust and various stubbornly resistant impurities from metal surfaces.

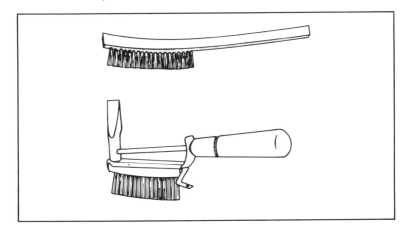

WOOD BENCH PIN: (See: V-BOARD WITH CLAMP).

WORKABILITY:
The characteristics which determine the ease of shaping a metal into desired configurations.

WORK ANGLE:
This is the angle at which the electrode is held during arc welding. For example, when a weld is made in flat position the electrode should be held at about a 15-degree angle to a line perpendicular to the weld axis at the weld point. The right angle will help the welder obtain a strong, smooth weld bead.

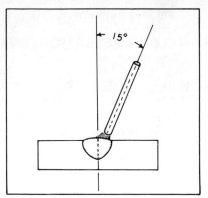

WORK LEAD:
The electric cable extending from a welding machine and current source to the work.

WROUGHT:
A general term referring to metals which may be hand-worked, hammered or beaten into shape with tools.

WROUGHT IRON:
The term "wrought iron" is currently used to refer to almost any malleable low carbon steel. Originally the term referred to a soft, workable iron having a carbon content of less than .03 percent. True wrought iron is scarce and expensive to buy today.

ZARI:
A form of embroidery that employs metallic gold and silver threads to decorate leather and cloth craft objects such as belts, handbags, or clothing.

ZEES:
A structural steel section which is similar in design to the letter "Z."

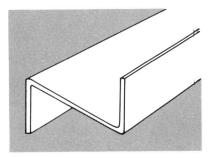

ZINC:
This metal is most commonly used by industry as a protective coating on steel and iron. Alloys of zinc are available in the form of wire, sheet, strips, foil and rods. Zinc is comparatively inexpensive but has moderate strength and toughness. Its low melting point, 420°C (787°F) makes zinc an excellent casting metal. Large quantities of zinc are used by the automobile and home appliance industry.

ZYGLO:
A fluorescent penetrant inspection technique for detecting flaws in nonmagnetic metals and solids.

TABLE I
METAL STOCK GUIDE

Names	Shapes	Length	How Measured	How Purchased
Angle		Lengths to 40 feet	Leg length x leg length x thickness of legs	Weight, foot or piece
Band		Lengths to 20 feet	Thickness x width	Weight or piece
Channel		Lengths to 60 feet	Depth x web thickness x flange width	Weight, foot or piece
Flats		Hot rolled 20-22 feet, cold finished	Thickness x width	Weight, foot or piece
Hexagon		12 to 20 feet lengths	Distance across flats	Weight, foot or piece

Shape		Length	Measurement	
I-Beam		Lengths to 60 feet	Height x web thickness x flange width	Weight, foot or piece
Octagon		12 to 20 foot lengths	Distance across flats	Weight, foot or piece
Plate (Over 1/4")		Lengths to 20 feet	Thickness x width	Weight, foot or piece
Rod		12 to 20 foot lengths	Diameter	Weight, foot or piece
Sheet (Less than 1/4")		Length to 144 inches	Thickness x width, widths to 72 inches	Weight, foot or piece
Square		12 to 20 foot lengths	Width	Weight, foot or piece

153

TABLE II
MELTING POINTS OF SELECTED METALS

Metal	Symbol	Melting Point		Melting Points Low to High Centigrade	
		Deg. C.	Deg. F.		
Aluminum (Cast)	Al	658	1217	Mercury	38.7
				Phosphorus	43
Aluminum (Rolled)	Al	-	-	Tin	232
				Bismuth	271
Antimony	Sb	630	1166	Cadmium	321
Bismuth	Bi	271	520	Lead	327
Cadmium	Cd	321	610	Zinc	419
Carbon	C	-	-	Antimony	630
Chromium	Cr	1510	2750	Magnesium	651
Cobalt	Co	1490	2714	Aluminum	658
Copper	Cu	1083	1982	Silver	961
Gold	Au	1063	1945	Gold	1063
Iridium	Ir	2300	4170	Copper	1083
Iron	Fe	1520	2768	Manganese	1225
Lead	Pb	327	621	Silicon	1427
Magnesium	Mg	651	1204	Nickel	1452
Manganese	Mn	1225	2237	Cobalt	1490
Mercury	Hg	-	-	Chromium	1510
Molybdenum	Mo	2620	4748	Iron	1520
Nickel	Ni	1452	2646	Vanadium	1730
Phosphorus	P	43	111.4	Platinum	1755
Platinum	Pt	1755	3191	Iridium	2300
Silicon	Si	1427	2600	Molybdenum	2620
Silver	Ag	961	1761	Tungsten	3000
Tin	Sn	232	450	Carbon	3500
Tungsten	W	3000	5432		
Vanadium	V	1730	3146		
Zinc	Zn	419	786		

TABLE III
Recommended Cutting Fluids and Drill Feed

Material to Be Drilled	Cutting Fluid(s)	Drill Feed
Aluminum and Alloys	Kerosene, Kerosene and Lard Oil, Soluble Oil	Medium
Brass and Bronze	Dry For Deep Holes: Kerosene and Mineral Oil, Lard Oil, Soluble Oil	Hard
Copper	Mineral Lard Oil and Kerosene, Soluble Oil, Dry	Light
Monel Metal	Mineral Lard Oil, Soluble Oil	Medium
Mild Steels	Mineral Oil, Soluble Oil	Hard
Tough Alloy Steels	Sulfurized Oils, Mineral Lard Oil	Medium
Steel Forgings	Sulfurized Oil, Mineral Lard Oil	L,M,H
Cast Steel	Soluble Oil, Sulfurized Oil	Light
Wrought Iron	Soluble Oil, Sulfurized Oil	Hard
High-Tensile Steels	Soluble Oil, Sulfurized Oil	Light
Manganese Steel	Dry	Light
Cast Iron	Dry	Light
Malleable Iron	Dry, Soluble Oil	Hard
Stainless Steel	Soluble Oil, Sulfurized Oil	Medium
Tool Steel	Mineral Lard Oil and Kerosene, Kerosene, Mineral Lard Oil	L,M,H

TABLE IV
TEMPERATURE CONVERSION
Fahrenheit to Centigrade

°F	°C	°F	°C	°F	°C	°F	°C	°F	°C	°F	°C	°F	°C
32	0	660	349	960	516	1260	682	1560	849	1880	1026	2180	1193
212	100	680	360	980	527	1280	693	1580	860	1900	1038	2200	1204
400	204	700	371	1000	538	1300	704	1600	871	1920	1049	2220	1216
420	216	720	382	1020	549	1320	716	1620	882	1940	1060	2240	1227
440	227	740	393	1040	560	1340	727	1640	893	1960	1071	2260	1238
460	238	760	404	1060	571	1360	738	1660	904	1980	1082	2280	1249
480	249	780	416	1080	582	1380	749	1680	916	2000	1093	2300	1260
500	260	800	427	1100	593	1400	760	1700	927	2020	1105	2320	1271
520	271	820	438	1120	604	1420	771	1740	949	2940	1116	2340	1284
540	282	840	449	1140	616	1440	782	1760	960	2060	1127	2360	1293
560	293	860	460	1160	627	1460	793	1780	971	2080	1138	2380	1305
580	304	880	471	1180	638	1480	804	1800	982	2100	1149	2400	1316
600	316	900	482	1200	649	1500	816	1820	993	2120	1160		
620	327	920	493	1220	660	1520	827	1840	1004	2140	1171		
640	338	940	504	1240	671	1540	838	1860	1015	2160	1182		

TABLE IV
(continued)

Centigrade to Fahrenheit

°C	°F	°C	°F	°C	°F	°C	°F	°C	°F	°C	°F	°C	°F
0	32	330	626	480	896	630	1166	780	1436	930	1706	1080	1976
100	212	340	644	490	914	640	1184	790	1454	940	1724	1090	1994
200	392	350	662	500	932	650	1202	800	1472	950	1742	1100	2012
210	410	360	680	510	950	660	1220	810	1490	960	1760	1110	2030
220	428	370	698	520	968	670	1238	820	1508	970	1778	1120	2048
230	446	380	716	530	986	680	1256	830	1526	980	1796	1130	2066
240	464	390	734	540	1004	690	1274	840	1544	990	1814	1140	2084
250	482	400	752	550	1022	700	1292	850	1562	1000	1832	1150	2102
260	500	410	770	560	1040	710	1310	860	1580	1010	1850	1160	2120
270	518	420	788	570	1058	720	1328	870	1598	1020	1868	1170	2138
280	536	430	806	580	1076	730	1346	880	1616	1030	1886	1180	2156
290	545	440	824	590	1094	740	1364	890	1634	1040	1904	1190	2174
300	572	450	842	600	1112	750	1382	900	1652	1050	1922		
310	590	460	860	610	1130	760	1400	910	1670	1060	1940		
320	608	470	878	620	1148	770	1418	920	1688	1070	1958		

Comparison of Thermometers
Freezing point=32° Fahrenheit= 0° Centigrade • Boiling point=212° Fahrenheit=100° Centigrade
$F = {}^9/_5C + 32°$, $C = {}^5/_9F -32°$

TABLE V

STANDARD FOR WIRE GAGES

(Dimensions of Sizes in Decimal Parts of an Inch)

Number of Wire Gage	American or Brown & Sharpe	Birmingham or Stubs' Iron Wire	Washburn & Moen, Worcester, Mass.	W. & M. Steel Music Wire	American S. & W. Co.'s Music Wire Gage	Imperial Wire Gage	Stubs' Steel Wire	U.S. Standard Gage for Sheet and Plate Iron and Steel	Number of Wire Gage
0000000				.0083					0000000
000000				.0087	.004	.464		.46875	000000
00000				.0095	.005	.432		.4375	00000
0000	.460	.454	.3938	.010	.006	.400		.40625	0000
000	.40964	.425	.3625	.011	.007	.372		.375	000
00	.3648	.380	.3310	.012	.008	.348		.34375	00
0	.32486	.340	.3065	.0133	.009	.324		.3125	0
1	.2893	.300	.2830	.0144	.010	.300	.227	.28125	1
2	.25763	.284	.2625	.0156	.011	.276	.219	.265625	2
3	.22942	.259	.2437	.0166	.012	.252	.212	.250	3
4	.20431	.238	.2253	.0178	.013	.232	.207	.234375	4
5	.18194	.220	.2070	.0188	.014	.212	.204	.21875	5
6	.16202	.203	.1920	.0202	.016	.192	.201	.203125	6
7	.14428	.180	.1770	.0215	.018	.176	.199	.1875	7
8	.12849	.165	.1620	.023	.020	.160	.197	.171875	8
9	.11443	.148	.1483	.0243	.022	.144	.194	.15625	9

10	.140625	.191	.128	.024	.027	.1350	.134	.10189
11	.125	.188	.116	.026	.0284	.1205	.120	.090742
12	.109375	.185	.104	.029	.0296	.1055	.109	.080808
13	.09375	.182	.092	.031	.0314	.0915	.095	.071961
14	.078125	.180	.080	.033	.0326	.0800	.083	.064084
15	.0703125	.178	.072	.035	.0345	.0720	.072	.057068
16	.0625	.175	.064	.037	.036	.0625	.065	.05082
17	.05625	.172	.056	.039	.0377	.0540	.058	.045257
18	.050	.168	.048	.041	.0395	.04575	.049	.040303
19	.04375	.164	.040	.043	.0414	.0410	.042	.03589
20	.0375	.161	.036	.045	.0434	.0348	.035	.031961
21	.034375	.157	.032	.047	.046	.03175	.032	.028462
22	.03125	.155	.028	.049	.0483	.0286	.028	.025347
23	.028125	.153	.024	.051	.051	.0258	.025	.022571
24	.025	.151	.022	.055	.055	.0230	.022	.0201
25	.021875	.148	.020	.059	.0586	.0204	.020	.0179
26	.01875	.146	.018	.063	.0626	.0181	.018	.01594
27	.0171875	.143	.0164	.067	.0658	.0173	.016	.014195
28	.015625	.139	.0149	.071	.072	.0162	.014	.012641
29	.0140625	.134	.0136	.075	.076	.0150	.013	.011257
30	.0125	.127	.0124	.080	.080	.0140	.012	.010025
31	.0109375	.120	.0116	.085	....	.0132	.010	.008928
32	.01015625	.115	.0108	.090	....	.0128	.009	.00795
33	.009375	.112	.0100	.095	....	.0118	.008	.00708
34	.00859375	.110	.0092	....	....	.0104	.007	.006304
35	.0078125	.108	.0084	....	....	.0095	.005	.005614
36	.00703125	.106	.0076	....	....	.0090	.004	.005
37	.00640625	.103	.0068	....	....	....	....	.004453
38	.00625	.101	.0060	....	....	....	....	.003965
39	....	.099	.0052	....	....	....	....	.003531
40	....	.097	.0048	....	....	....	....	.003144

TABLE VI

COMMON ELECTRODE WELDING GUIDE

Rod	Type of Current	Polarity	Position	Flux Coating	% Iron Powder
E6010	DC	Reverse	All	Cellulose-sodium	0-10
E6011	AC or DC	Reverse	All	Cellulose-potassium	0
E6012	AC or DC	Straight	All	Rutile-sodium	0-10
E6013	AC or DC	Either	All	Rutile-potassium	0-10
E6014	AC or DC	Either	All	Rutile-iron powder	25-40
*E6015	DC	Reverse	All	Low-hydrogen-sodium	0
*E6016	AC or DC	Straight	All	Low-hydrogen-potassium	0
*E6018	AC or DC	Reverse	All	Low-hydrogen-iron powder	25-40
E6020	AC or DC	Straight	Flat or Horizontal	Iron oxide-sodium	0
E6024	AC or DC	Either	Flat or Horizontal	Rutile-iron powder	50
E6027	AC or DC	Either	Flat or Horizontal	Iron oxide-iron powder	50
*E6028	AC or DC	Reverse	Flat or Horizontal	Low-hydrogen-iron powder	50
E6030	AC or DC	Straight	Flat	Iron oxide	

*Low-Hydrogen Rods

Suppliers of Metals and Metalworking Tools and Equipment

Allcraft Tool and Supply Co., Inc.
100 Frank Road
Hicksville, New York 11801
(Metalworking and jewelers tools and supplies)

Arcos Corporation
1500 South 50th Street
Philadelphia, PA 19143
(Welding electrodes, wire and fluxes)

Axel Johnson and Co., Inc. (Avesta)
680 East Swedesford Road
P.O. Box 431
Wayne, Pennsylvania 19087
(Stainless steel welding products)

Belmont Metals Inc., Division of Belmont Smelting and Refining
320 Belmont Avenue
Brooklyn, N.Y. 11207
(All Metal alloys)

Brodhead-Garrett Co.
4560 East 71st Street
Cleveland, Ohio 44105
(Metalworking and shop tools and equipment)

Buffalo Forge Company
490 Broadway
Buffalo, New York 14241
(Forges, blowers and accessories)

Forge and Anvil
1200 Crest Valley Drive NW
Atlanta, Georgia 30327
(Forging equipment)

Gold Leaf and Metallic Powders, Inc.
Two Barclay Street
New York, N.Y. 10007
(Gold leaf)

Graves-Humphreys, Inc.
1948 Franklin Road
P.O. Box 13407
Roanoke, VA 24033
(Metalworking and shop tools and equipment)

Handy and Harman
850-A Third Avenue
New York, N.Y. 10022
(All forms of precious metals)

Hobart Brothers Company
Box EW-464
Troy, Ohio 45373
(Welding supplies and equipment)

International Nickel Co., Inc.
One N.Y. Plaza, Dept. T
New York, N.Y. 10004
(Nickel alloys)

Julius Blum and Company, Inc.
P.O. Box 292
Carlstadt, New Jersey 07072
(Architectural and ornamental metal components)

Leach and Garner Co.
James and Pearl Streets
Attleboro, MA 02703
(Gold, silver, gold-filled and laminated metals)

Lenco, Inc.
319 West Main Street
Jackson, MO 63755
(Welding Products)

Linde Company
Union Carbide Corporation
Linde, Division, Fifth Floor
270 Park Avenue
New York, N.Y. 10017
(Complete welding tools and equipment)

Manhattan Aluminum Corp.
56-71 49th Street
Maspeth, N.Y. 11378
(Aluminum)

Manhattan Brass and Copper Co., Inc.
56-71 49th Street
Maspeth, N.Y. 11378
(Copper alloys)

161

McEnglevan Heat Treating & Manufacturing Co.
P.O. Box 31, 700 Griggs Street
Danville, IL 61832
  (Casting furnaces and accessories)

Metal Powder & Chem. Works Inc.
225 Broadway
New York, N.Y. 10007
  (Gold leaf and metallic powders)

Norton Company
#1 New Bond Street
Worcester, MA 01606
  (Abrasives, grinding wheels)

Olin Mathieson Chemical Corp.
Metals Division
120 Long Ridge Road
Stamford, CT 06904
  (Aluminum Information)

Revere Copper and Brass, Inc.
605 Third Avenue
New York, N.Y. 10016
  (Copper alloys)

Roper Whitney, Inc.
2833 Huffman Blvd.
Rockford, IL 61101
  (Manually operated punches, benders,
  notchers, and shears)

T. E. Conklin Brass and Copper Co., Inc.
322-324 West 23rd Street
New York, N.Y. 10011
  (Copper alloys)

Selected Bibliography

General Metalworking (Theoretical and Technical)

Adams, Jeannette T., *Metalworking Handbook,* New York: Arco Publishing, 1976.

Aluminum Development Council of Australia (Ltd). Aluminum Technology, Book Six, *Casting Aluminum,* 1974.

American Foundrymen's Society, *Shell Process Foundry Practice,* Des Plaines, IL 1973.

American Iron and Steel Institute, *Designer's Handbook: Steel Wire,* Washington, D.C., 1974.

Braun-Feldwig, Wilheim, *Metal Design and Technique,* New York: Van Nostrand Reinhold Co., 1975.

Bureau of Naval Personnel, *Tools and Their Uses,* New York: Dover Publications, Inc., 1973.

Chaplin, Jack W., *Metal Manufacturing Technology,* Bloomington, Ill.: McKnight Publishing Co., 1976.

Halsted Division, John Wiley and Sons, *Foundry Technology,* New York, 1972.

Kratfel, Edward R., *Introduction to Modern Sheet Metal,* Reston, VA: Reston Publishing Co., Inc., 1976.

Kuhn, F., *Decorative Work in Wrought Iron and Other Metals,* New York: Hastings House, 1977.

Maryon, Herbert, *Metalwork and Enameling: A Practical Treatise on Gold and Silversmith's Work and their Allied Crafts,* London: Chapman and Hall, 1959.

Meilach, Dona, *Decorative and Sculptural Ironwork,* New York: Crown Publishers, Inc., 1977.

Parmley, R. O. (Editor), *Standard Handbook of Fastening and Joining,* New York: McGraw-Hill Book Co., 1977.

Ross, Robert B., *Handbook of Metal Treatments and Testing,* New York: Halsted Press, 1977.

Schwarzkopf, Ernst, *Plain and Ornamental Forging,* London: John Wiley & Sons, Inc., 1916.

Ullrich, Heinz and Klante, Dieter, *Creative Metal Design,* New York: Reinhold Book Corp., 1968.

163

Untracht, Oppi, *Metal Techniques for Craftsmen,* New York: Doubleday & Co., Inc., 1975.

Walker, John R., *Modern Metalworking, Materials, Tools and Procedures,* South Holland, Ill.: The Goodheart-Willcox Co., Inc., 1976.

Walton, C. F. (Editor), *Grey and Ductile Iron Castings Handbook,* Cleveland, Ohio: Grey and Ductile Iron Founder's Society Inc., 1971.

Welding and Soldering

Althouse, A. D., Turnquist, C. H. and Bowditch, W. A., *Modern Welding,* South Holland, Ill.: The Goodheart-Willcox Co., Inc., 1976.

American Society for Metals, *Metals Handbook,* 8th Edition, Volume 6, (Welding and Brazing), Metals Park, Ohio, 1971.

American Welding Society, *Welding Handbook,* 7th Edition, Volume 1, (Fundamentals of Welding), Miami, Fla., 1976.

American Welding Society, *Welding Handbook,* 7th Edition, Volume 2, (Welding Processes: Arc and Gas Welding and Cutting, Brazing and Soldering), Miami, Fla., 1978.

American Welding Society, *Brazing Manual,* 3rd Edition, Miami, Florida, 1976.

American Welding Society, *Soldering Manual,* 2nd Edition, Miami, Florida, 1978.

American Welding Society, *Microworld of Joining Technology,* New York, 1969.

Baird, R. J., *Oxyacetylene Welding: Basic Fundamentals,* South Holland, Ill.: The Goodheart-Willcox Co., Inc., 1977.

Burke, John J., *Advances in Joining Technology,* Chestnut Hill, Mass.: Brook Hill Publishing Co., 1976.

Davies, A. C., *Science and Practice of Welding,* 7th Edition, Cambridge University Press, 1977.

Frankland, Thomas W., *The Pipe Fitter's and Pipe Welder's Handbook,* Beverly Hills, California: Benziger, Bruce and Glencoe, Inc., 1969.

Giachino, J. W. and Weeks, W., *Welding Skills and Practices,* 5th Edition, Chicago, Ill: American Technical Society, 1976.

Griffin, I. H. and Roden, E. M., *Basic TIG and MIG Welding,* Albany, N. Y.: Delmar Publishers Inc., 1971.

Griffin, I. H., Roden E. M., and Briggs, C. W., *Basic Welding Techniques: Three Books in One: Arc; Oxyacetylene; MIG and TIG,* London: Van Nostrand Reinhold, 1977.

Griffin, I. H., Roden, E. M. and Briggs, C. W., *Basic (Manual Metal) Arc Welding,* 3rd Edition, Albany, N.Y.: Delmar Publishers, 1977.

Hobart Brothers Company, *Pocket Welding Guide,* 21st Edition, Troy, Ohio, 1977.

Houldcroft, P. T., *Welding Process Technology,* London: Cambridge University Press, 1977.

Jefferson, T. B. and Woods, Gorham, *Metals and How to Weld Them,* Cleveland, Ohio: The James F. Lincoln Arc Welding Foundation, 2nd Edition, 1962.

Jefferson, T. B., *The Oxy-acetylene Weldor's Handbook,* Lake Zurich, Illinois: Monticello Books, Inc., 7th Edition, 1972.

Johnston, B. G., and Lin, F. J., *Basic Steel Design,* Englewood Cliffs, N. J.: Prentice-Hall, Inc., 1974.

Kennedy, Gower A., *Welding Technology,* Indianapolis: Howard W. Sams & Co., Inc., 1974.

Lincoln Arc Welding Foundation, *Modern Welded Constructions,* Cleveland, Ohio: James F. Lincoln Arc Welding Foundation, 1969.

Lincoln Arc Welding Foundation, *Modern Welded Structures,* Cleveland, Ohio: James F. Lincoln Arc Welding Foundation, 1963.

Lincoln Electric Company, *Handbook of Arc Welding,* 12th Edition, Cleveland, Ohio: The Lincoln Electric Co., 1973.

Lindberg, R. A. and Braton, N. R., *Welding and Other Joining Processes,* Boston: Allyn and Bacon, 1976.

Little, R. L., *Welding and Welding Technology,* New York: McGraw-Hill Book Company, 1973.

Masson, F. N., *Welding, Theory and Practice,* Macmillan Company of Canada, Ltd., 1967.

Nikolaev, G. and Olshansky, N., *Advanced Welding Processes,* Moscow: MIR Publishers, 1977.

Patton, W. J., *The Science and Practice of Welding,* Englewood Cliffs, N.J.: Prentice-Hall, Inc., 1967.

Smith, F. J., *Basic Fabrication and Welding Engineering,* London: Longman, 1975.

Thwaites, C. J., *Soft-Soldering Handbook,* Greenford-Middlesex: International Tin Research Institute, 1977.

Union Carbide Corporation, *MIG Welding Handbook,* New York: Linde Division, Union Carbide Corp., 1974.

Union Carbide Corporation, *Submerged Arc Welding Handbook,* New York: Linde Division, Union Carbide Corp., 1974.

Walker, John R., *Arc Welding: Basic Fundamentals,* South Holland, Ill.: The Goodheart-Willcox Co., Inc., 1977.

165

Metal Sculpture:

Baldwin, John, *Contemporary Sculpture Techniques,* New York: Reinhold Publishing Corporation, 1967.

Benton, Suzanne, *The Art of Welded Sculpture,* New York: Van Nostrand Reinhold Co., 1975.

Hale, Nathan Cabot, *Welded Sculpture,* New York: Watson-Guptill Pub., 1968.

Hauser, C., *Art Foundry,* Geneva: Editions De Bonvent, 1972.

Irving, Donald J., *Sculpture Material and Process,* New York: Van Nostrand Reinhold Co., 1970.

Meilach, Dona and Seiden, Don, *Direct Metal Sculpture,* New York: Crown Publishers, Inc., 1966.

Morris, John D., *Creative Metal Sculpture,* New York: The Bruce Publishing Company, 1971.

Rood, John, *Sculpture With A Torch,* Minneapolis, Minn.: University of Minnesota Press, 1963.

Verheist, Wilbert, *Sculpture: Tools, Materials and Techniques,* New Jersey: Prentice-Hall, Inc., 1973.

Withers, J., *Julio Gonzales: Sculpture In Iron,* New York: New York University Press, 1977.

Historical:

Biringuccio, Vannoccio, *The Pirotechnica (De La Pirotechnica),* Venice, 1540. English translation by Cyril S. Smith and Martha T. Gnudi, The American Institute of Mining and Metallurgical Engineers, Inc., 1942.

Cellini, Benvenuto, *Treaties on Goldsmithing and Sculpture,* 16th Century. Translated by C. R. Ashbee, 1898.

Cennini, Cennino D'Andrea, *The Craftsman's Handbook,* 15th Century. Translated by Daniel V. Thompson, Jr., New York: Dover Publications, 1963.

Forbes, R. J., *Studies in Ancient Technology,* Leiden, Netherlands: E. J. Brill, Vol. 8 and 9, 1964.

Hatcher, T., and Barker, T. C., *A History of British Pewter,* London: Longman, 1974.

Hover, Otto, *Wrought Iron: Encyclopedia of Ironwork*, New York: Universe Books, 1962.

Kerfoot, J. B., *American Pewter*, Detroit, Michigan: Gale Research Co., 1976.

Kolchin, B. A., *Metallurgy and Metal Working in Ancient Russia*, Jerusalem: S. Monson, 1967.

Montgomery, C. F., *A History of American Pewter*, New York: Praeger, 1973.

Robertson, E. G. and Robertson, J., *Cast Iron Decoration:* A World Survey, London: Thames and Hudson, 1977.

Simonson, R. D., *The History of Welding*, Morton Grove, Ill: Monticello Books, Inc., 1969.

Street, Arthur C., *Metals in The Service of Man*, Baltimore, Penguin Books, 1972.

Theophilus, Presbyter (Roger of Helmarshausen), *De Diversis Artibus (The Various Arts)*, 12th Century. Translated by C. R. Dodwell, London: Thomas Nelson and Sons Ltd., 1961.

Vasari, Georgio, *Vasari On Technique*, 1550. Translated by Louisa S. MacLehose. New York: Dover Publications, 1960.

Zimelli, Umberto and Vergerio, Giovanni, *Decorative Ironwork*, London: The Hamlyn Publishing Group Limited, 1969.

167